A Month of Mondays

God didn't go to all the trouble of sending his Son
merely to point an accusing finger,
telling the world how bad it was.
He came to help,
to put the world right again.

JOHN 3:16-17 (*The Message*)

A MONTH OF MONDAYS

Spiritual Lessons from the Catholic Classroom

KAREN EIFLER

FOREWORD BY PATRICK HANNON, CSC

A MONTH OF MONDAYS
Spiritual Lessons from the Catholic Classroom
by Karen Eifler
with a Foreword by Patrick Hannon, CSC

Edited by Gregory F. Augustine Pierce
Cover by Tom A. Wright
Text design and typesetting by Patricia A. Lynch

Published by ACTA Publications, 4848 N. Clark Street, Chicago, IL 60640, (800) 397-2282, www.actapublications.com

Library of Congress Catalog number: 2011920358
ISBN: 978-0-87946-456-1
Printed in the United States of America by Evangel Press
Year 20 19 18 17 16 15 14 13 12 11
Printing 15 14 13 12 11 10 9 8 7 6 5 4 3 2 First

♻ Text printed on 30% post-consumer recycled paper

Contents

Foreword by Patrick Hannon, CSC / 9

Introduction / 13

A Few Things Left to Learn / 15

God Bless Mrs. Bigelow / 19

Taking the God's Eye View / 23

God Can Work Any Miracle / 27

Check, Check, Check / 31

A Word We All Need / 35

The Communion of Saints / 39

Those Crazy Present-Tense Beatitudes / 43

Asked and Half-Asked / 47

Be Loved /51

Least Favorite Student /55

I Teach People, Not Geography / 59

Probing Their Wounds / 63

Picture Day / 67

The Power of the Personal / 71

Written on the Heart / 75

On "Not Working" / 79

Tell It Slant / 83

The Tongue of a Teacher / 87

Weaving Crowns of Verbal Thorns / 91

"Inverted Jenny" Students / 95

Getting It Righter / 99

Hoping Boldly /103

Waging Peace One Email at a Time /107

Good Samaritans / 111

The Grace of Vulnerability / 115

Ninety-Nine Times Out of Ten / 119

The Rockets' Red Glare /123

Bury as Useful / 127

Falling in Love Again / 131

Acknowledgments / 135

For Mark,
In gratitude for rainbows
All the days of my life

Foreword

Jumping Out of Our Own Skin

BY PATRICK HANNON, CSC

Andrew Simon was a student I taught years ago at Notre Dame High School for Boys outside of Chicago, Illinois. He sat in the fourth row second seat in my freshman Introduction to Literature and Composition class. He stood four feet ten and weighed in at a scrawny ninety pounds by my reckoning. He wore thick-rimmed glasses and slacks that exposed white socks tucked into oversized penny loafers. I recall our first encounter. He came rushing into my classroom a minute late on the first day of class carrying all of his textbooks. He found the last open desk, dropped his books with a thud on the desk top, slid into the seat, retrieved a handkerchief from his pocket, wiped his sweaty brow, and said, "Jesus Christ, it's a frickin' mile from the gym to here!" Only he didn't say *frickin'*. He opened his notebook, retrieved a pen from his shirt pocket, clicked it open, licked the tip, and wrote the date at the top left hand corner of the blank page. With that he took a deep breath, exhaled, looked up, and stared at me.

Burdened with Asperger's Syndrome—a high-functioning form of autism—Andrew was an awkward boy. He was prone to odd ticks and sudden outbursts and peculiar habits of being. He rarely smiled. Watching him as he sat in class, a thoughtful observer would note a level of concentration rare in a thirteen-year-old. It was as if he had harnessed every last bit of energy in his body for the sole purpose of keeping himself from jumping out of his own skin. And sometimes he simply failed at that task. One day, for instance, Tom, who sat directly behind Andrew, began poking Andrew's back with his pen. Tom hadn't an ounce of guile in him; he had simply drifted off into some daydream and was absentmindedly poking the nearest warm body. The class was quiet at the time. And then Andrew leaped out of his seat, swung around to face a startled Tom, and said in frantic voice, "Smith, if, if, if you don't stop poking me with that frickin' pen, I'm going to kick your, your, your…ASS." Only he didn't say *frickin'*.

Andrew Simon's classmates loved him. I loved him. Everyone loved him, and for all the right reasons. He was exasperating and entertaining. He was thoughtful and provocative. He tantalized us and amazed us. He challenged us and stretched the boundaries of propriety and dared us to accept him as he was. In short, Andrew Simon was for his classmates and me an instrument of grace. I had only one conversation with my freshmen about Andrew early on, and it was in his absence. I spelled out for them the particularities of Asperger's and simply asked them to be patient with him. Patient they were. In his own way, Andrew the student became Andrew the teacher, drawing out of us skills and competencies we always had hoped we harbored. The Andrew Simon Lesson Plan—no less real or understood for being unspoken—brought every person in the class, myself included, to a deeper experience of our own (often hidden) fragile humanity, to a crossroads where compassion and hope and understanding intersected.

Andrew was one of the brightest students I ever taught. On my challenge, he read James Joyce's *Ulysses*, for crying out loud, and then offered me a ten-paged, typed, written critique of it! But what I remember now is what he extracted from me, his teacher, and from his classmates. He brought out the best in us. Even as I attempted to instill a thirst for excellence in my students, he planted in me the desire to be good and loving.

But he probably never knew it. Andrew was too busy trying to keep himself from jumping out of his own skin.

To me, this is what teaching is all about and why you simply must read every story in this book. Karen Eifler, a teacher of teachers (and thus a student at heart), gives us here a glimpse of the teacher's soul. She rightly suggests that we teachers harbor the hope that someday we will become an instrument of grace, a conduit of hope for our students, when in truth most days we are busy just trying to keep ourselves from jumping out of our own skin. In this we share a kind of comradeship with loving parents, who—like all great teachers—spill their blood daily for their tyke or teen or young adult.

But even as they are keeping their body and soul together, great teachers also are forming minds and hearts. They are creating and crafting and conjuring and cajoling. They extract holiness from tiny hearts and make them bigger. They coax greatness out of shy shadows. Every Monday during the school year, teachers hoist themselves from weekend slumber, put on their best face, and, fortified by caffeine and a holy lunacy, go to meet their capacious students at the crossroads of hope and compassion and understanding. It is at this intersection where real teaching happens.

With a nimble mind, a loving heart, a gentle wit, and a master teacher's keen and perceptive eye, Karen Eifler has captured the *essence* of the teaching craft: to help students become—without their ever realizing it is happening—clever, skillful practitioners of hope. Woven throughout this "Month of Mondays" is an insistence that all the virtues that mark a life worth living are not acquired easily. Like our students, we teachers *become* graceful and loving, smart and wise, generous and kind *because* we ourselves had great teachers both inside and outside the classroom. And Karen Eifler is one of them.

Introduction

"You'll be telling the stories for all those amazing teachers who never get to tell theirs! Who ever thinks of grammar school and middle school and high school kids as occasions of grace?" So said my friend Father Pat Hannon when he challenged me to put this collection together.

What you will encounter here are thirty snapshots of grace in action, enough to fill "a month of Mondays" for busy teachers, administrators, and catechists. Each story is preceded by a verse from Scripture or other sacred texts, to serve as an anchor for a contemplative reading of the day's tale. While I've changed their names, out of respect for privacy and to allow quiet space for their continued miracle-working, these true stories are rendered to provide living illustrations of my favorite image in poetry, from Gerard Manley Hopkins' "As Kingfishers Catch Fire":

> ...Christ plays in ten thousand places,
> Lovely in limbs, and lovely in eyes not his
> To the Father through the features of men's faces.

Ours is a God of surprises, sometimes even playfulness, and the teachers celebrated in these stories are ever aware of God's capacity to unleash grace on them, sometimes in a trickle, sometimes in a flood, always through the students, parents, and colleagues who move through their classrooms.

Each story invites teachers to reflect on the miracles they themselves will be working that day and the faces and limbs of Christ they will encounter that day in their classrooms, even on Mondays.

Karen Eifler
Portland, Oregon
January 2011

A Few Things Left to Learn

Let no one despise your youth,
but set the believers an example
in speech and conduct,
in love,
in faith,
in purity.

1 TIMOTHY 4:12

R aw meat. That's how eighth graders usually see a new teacher, especially one with no experience, like me on that February Monday when I took on the very first class that would become "mine."

I'd gotten the job offer a week earlier from the interim principal, who was only hours into her own new role. Miss Wood had been the eighth-grade teacher there since the earth was cooling and enjoyed the respect and trust of the school and parish community. She was really going to need both as word trickled out that the old principal was suddenly gone (and why) and that Miss Wood was now in charge.

Like many parochial schools, tuition only paid part of the bills; students and their parents were constantly selling wrapping paper and cupcakes and doodads to pay for frills such as current textbooks. The most recent fundraiser had been wildly successful. Even two weeks after it was over, classroom closets housed the lingering aroma of the mountains of chocolate bars students had hustled, netting over ten thousand dollars.

Now, ten thousand dollars, stacked in mounds of mostly singles, is a lot of money. Enough, as it turned out, to finance a one-way plane ticket to Mexico and plush accommodations for the previous principal, who took the candy money, along with an assumed name, and set up a new life for himself on a sunny beach south of the border, creating an immediate job vacancy.

God speaks to people in a multitude of ways: a burning bush, a rainbow, a rushing wind, the gentlest of breezes. Or, in my case, through grand larceny. Because it turns out that teaching is exactly what I am supposed to be doing, and I got to start doing it because Miss Wood became principal over the weekend and needed someone to take over her eighth graders on very short notice. She knew of me because I had conducted a one-day Confirmation retreat for her class, and she had been impressed that they could not make me cry in the course of our eight hours together. Not crying was apparently the main thing she was looking for in a candidate to finish out the school year in this toughish Los Angeles Catholic elementary school.

That I could also play six chords on the guitar meant the brand new principal had also just gained a liturgical music leader for the school, and when she found out I had once purchased my college roommate's calculus book back from her as a favor, I obviously had the credentials to teach math for grades six through eight. (Catholic schools are notorious for drawing out gifts and talents that people don't know they have.)

I got the job and took the week between the job offer and first class bell to read everything I could on classroom management. In my newbie mind, I was getting off to a strong start and making Miss Wood's classroom my own.

The pedagogical literature in those days was adamant that teachers had to project exactly who was boss from their initial contact with their students. Dressing professionally was key, according to the books, and I agonized in selecting clothes that communicated authority and business tempered by just the tiniest dash of approachability. In the mirror I practiced the withering Teacher Look I would eventually patent.

I put *The Trouble with Angels* movie on infinite loop and prayed to channel Rosalind Russell's Mother Superior from that film. Same with Sidney Poitier's Mr. Thackeray in *To Sir, With Love.*

I made my list of non-negotiable rules.

The bulletin boards were masterpieces.

I was ready; bring it on, Monday!

Monday brought it on, all right. I was the first person on the premises, radiating the loftiest of expectations in my pacing up and down the playground on high heels I had to force not to wobble. I could feel the eyes of hundreds of children burning into me, and I was pretty sure I saw several of the older boys rubbing their hands together in anticipatory glee at the torture they would soon be inflicting on "The New Teacher." But I almost felt sorry for them; I was that ready.

The girls were subtler, as they always are. Most of the action came from their eyes, a slow up and down as they took my measure. I was ready for them too.

The morning bell rang; time to commence my teaching career. I had also been working on my Teacher Voice, so it was loud and clear as these, the first words I ever spoke in public as a professional educator, roared out of my mouth on the playground: *"Boys, grab your balls and line up now! I mean it!"*

God would be with me in the days and weeks to come, helping me understand I still had a few things to learn about teaching.

I still do.

God Bless Mrs. Bigelow

Listen carefully, my son,
to the master's instructions,
and attend to them
with the ear of your heart.

PROLOGUE TO THE RULE OF ST. BENEDICT

Mrs. Bigelow wasn't just the world's best kindergarten teacher; she was a pretty fine theologian—the best kind. She taught about God subconsciously, and with every fiber of her being.

The first two words Mrs. Bigelow always taught the little souls who showed up in her classroom for forty-seven years were "Look!" and "Listen!" She might not literally have used the exclamation points, but they were always in her voice. Because in her gentle way, Mrs. Bigelow was always reminding children to keep their eyes and ears open. Every year, her students saw miracles, heard miracles, drew their distracted parents into the world of miracles.

Echoing Mrs. Bigelow at home one day, Conor Flynn let out with an exuberant "Look, Mom!" as he showed her a caterpillar. Conor helped his mother behold the velvet as she ran her finger over the caterpillar's back. So very soft it was, wriggling on Conor's palm as he held it out reverently, insistently to her. It took the mother back to another velvet, the kind that had first covered her newborn son's head, and she let her hand linger on the hair of this rambunctious five-year-old version of that miracle. How long would it be before he would pull away from that motherly gesture, or be embarrassed when she held his hand crossing the street?

For now, however, thanks to Mrs. Bigelow, Mom was reminded it was important to "Look!" and so she did, stroking Conor's head as he gently did the same with his caterpillar.

"Listen, Dad!" Courtney Flynn, Conor's twin sister, insisted, as she and her father sat on their back porch swing one balmy summer evening sucking their Popsicles (red for him, purple for her). He did listen, and, sure enough there were the blasted crickets. Dad added "buy bug spray" to the mental list of chores requiring his attention. All he needed was an infestation of crickets in the basement.

But Courtney heard things differently. "Listen to that music! That kinda sounds like a symphony warming up before a concert, doesn't it, Dad?"

Jeezaloo, thought the dad, when did this little mite they'd propped up next to a sack of sugar for her "Baby's First Christmas" photo get big enough to require her own Popsicle? Wasn't it just yesterday they had been splitting one (loser got the side with the chunk missing)? And now he was teaching her how to avoid Popsicle "brain freeze" and that reds and purples really, truly taste better than greens and oranges—same as with Skittles and M&M's.

If he wasn't careful, pretty soon her little scuffed-up legs would be long enough to touch the porch floor, and his daughter would be swinging herself and not need him to do it for her. Worse, Courtney might even go from wearing her mom's high heels at playtime "Dress Up" to wearing them for real to a school dance. Or to her own wedding.

And so the father took his daughter's hand, snuggled in a bit closer, and listened to the crickets as she instructed him to. They listened as Mrs. Bigelow had taught her, and—sure enough—for a while he could hear their symphony.

Mastering letters and numbers and how to line up quietly and play nicely with others are the absolute bedrock skills of "doing school," but sometimes we teachers forget that our sophomores are able to read *A Midsummer Night's Dream* and our Honors Math students can solve vector calculus problems only because a heroic early childhood teacher, or perhaps a team of them, labored before us to help little ones crack the code of looking and listening.

To feel velvet on a caterpillar's back, to hear music in a cricket's hum—these only happen when the Mrs. Bigelows of the world insist that the first lesson we must learn is to *Look!* and to *Listen!*

Taking the God's Eye View

Save me, O God,
for the waters have come up to my neck.

PSALM 69:1

"Richard, I really need you to stop slam-dunking Baby Jesus."
Now *there* is a sentence I never expected to hear myself
saying, let alone at the top of my exasperated-teacher
lungs. But here we were, in dress rehearsal for the world's most
ambitious Christmas pageant of all time, and Richard was driving
me crazy.

You have to believe there is a special tier of plush chaise
lounges and frosty umbrella drinks served by personal masseuses
reserved in heaven for music teachers who are truly convinced
it is possible to put together a ninety-minute Christmas show
featuring all three-hundred-plus students in grades kindergarten
through eight. This year's extravaganza by Miss Johnson rather
inexplicably wove together the antics of a traveling circus (allowing precious turns by adorable kinders and first graders as tum-
blers, animals, and clowns) with visitors to the circus (cue the
ever-trustworthy middle graders), somehow culminating in the
Nativity at Bethlehem, to be presented reverently by my eighth
graders. By some cosmic joke of a lottery, Richard had been chosen to portray Joseph, to the humiliated horror of Emily, as his
espoused wife Mary.

Very few days went by without Richard fully illuminating for me the gaps between the theory and practice of classroom management. Spitwads? Rookie stuff for him. Richard was the one who introduced me to the lethal power of dried lentils blown with devastating accuracy silently and swiftly through hollowed-out Bic pen casings. When the class made origami cranes to bring to life the well-known story of Sadako and the Ten Thousand Cranes in a special liturgy dedicated to the world's peacemakers, Richard organized a cadre of boys to turn their cranes into mutants. (When you think about it, that Richardian effort was impressive, as origami is challenging stuff to begin with, and *mutant* origami takes serious thought and dexterity.) And Richard argued compellingly that the atomic blast that triggered Sadako's story in the first place would have resulted in a lot of malformations among waterfowl, so he was just being truthful...and "shouldn't we always be truthful, especially when we are praying, Miz Eifler?"

Richard was like that: impenetrably logical answers for every conceivable infraction. Take his approach to the school's DEAR reading campaign, for instance, where every person in the entire building was to "Drop Everything and Read" for thirty uninterrupted minutes after lunch, working their way through several genres by the end of the year, the idea being to nourish in each student the pleasurable habit of reading a variety of literature. Well, Richard was a big Stephen King fan. Challenged on his relentless ingesting of those gory books and told to diversify, he made cogent arguments for how King is at home in multiple genres: mystery, science fiction, contemporary realistic. And since he was totally absorbed for that half hour each day, tormenting no one, Richard made me grateful that most of Stephen King's books clock in at a thousand pages or more, and that King is among our generation's most prolific authors.

So there we were in the cafegymatorium of the school for the final run-through of the Christmas pageant. It wasn't just Richard; none of the eighth graders were responding well to my pleas to set a good example for the younger students. I was admittedly hard-pressed to help them understand the tenuous narrative thread that wove together the traveling circus subplot with the Mystery of the Incarnation that would crown the evening.

No matter how hard we tried, the children could not remember the order of the verses for our assigned song, "Do You Hear What I Hear?" On their best days, eighth graders as a group feel like a herd of huge honking zits. Adding the boredom of a four-hour rehearsal and increasingly justified fears of looking silly in front of the evening's audience was just too much for most of them. Better to be seen as rebellious than as incompetent, I guess.

So, here's what happened. "Joseph" lateraled the doll from the manger to Kyle. Kyle popped it over his shoulder to Jimmy, one of the shepherds, who did not seem at all sore afraid as he lobbed it back to Richard, who executed a magnificent lay-up, nothing but net, through the basketball hoop at the end of the court. To his credit as Protector, Richard caught the doll almost tenderly. They ran the sequence again. And again. And again. Until I had to step in and confiscate our Baby Jesus with my screaming admonition.

Of course we all got through the performance magnificently. How could it be otherwise, with an audience full of parents and grandparents beaming as they watched the most precious people in their worlds onstage? Even the Three Wise Guys (as I will forever refer to them) searched the crowd during their bows and bestowed sheepishly proud grins on their personal cheering sections.

And that was what I had to learn from enduring the slam-dunk contest leading up to that pageant: every student, even the ones who trigger unknown reservoirs of hair-pulling rage inside me, are loved passionately by somebody. It's always a game-changer when I look at my students that way. One of my other wise friends calls it "taking the God's eye view."

GOD CAN WORK ANY MIRACLE

Truly I tell you,
unless you change and become like children,
you will never enter the kingdom of heaven.

MATTHEW 18:3

Mrs. Bigelow, the kindergarten teacher, wasn't just amazing with her kindergartners. She also brought out the gooey marshmallow center in even the most callused eighth graders.

One day my class was reminiscing about how magical life had been in kindergarten and how, at their ripe old age of thirteen or fourteen, they really missed believing in Santa Claus. Those with little brothers and sisters expressed a sweet concern that their siblings were somehow missing out on the sparkly holiday fantasy of believing that Santa would listen to whatever a five-year-old said, as long as it was sincere.

Operation Christmas Magic was born.

Richard had the most magical idea of all. Yes, this was the same Richard who shot lentils at Becca and Julianne through a hollowed-out Bic pen casing and slam-dunked the Baby Jesus during the school Christmas pageant rehearsal. But he came up with the idea that we all write letters *from* Santa *to* the kindergartners. He proclaimed that anyone could *answer* a letter from a kid to Santa, but the real trick would be in revealing what life is like at the North Pole without having to worry about dodging specific gift requests. "We shouldn't have our letters focus on presents anyway; that's not what Christmas is all about," Richard reminded us as he made his proposal. He'd obviously thought this through.

We wouldn't just write on any old paper, he suggested, but on ice blue paper, the color of the Arctic Circle. And we'd use special ink. In a flash, like a playful twist on the story of the wedding at Cana, hidden stores of glitter pens, along with a surprising assortment of stickers and rubber stamps, appeared from eighth-grade backpacks, enhancing the stodgy blue and black pens ordinarily demanded in my formal writing assignments.

Richard procured a class list from Mrs. Bigelow and matched each of his classmates with one of her students. He even ran a brainstorming session, a genuine pre-writing sequence that covered the board with multi-sensory prompts and adjectives that detonated the most reluctant writers. I had never seen Richard like this before, and I liked what I saw.

Suddenly, visions of my students meeting their state creative writing proficiency requirements danced in my head. Students who were usually surly about revising their assignments developed multiple drafts and started over, not just changing a word here and there, but coming up with new (and mostly better) concepts. They checked out thesauruses, labored over their spelling and penmanship on this one (because, duh, of course *elves* would write in their own hands and not leave such a precious task to the cold impersonality of a computer).

These were writers with an authentic audience, and they did not want to let their little buddies down. Richard's next stroke of genius was to spritz each paper with a mister and put them in the faculty lounge freezer until ice formed (which of course it would on any letters fresh from the North Pole).

On the afternoon the letters were to arrive at the kindergarten, Richard first took a string of jingle bells and made some surreptitious passes by the classroom, shaking the bells gently each time. No one was better cut out for a stealth task such as this. He was the master at not getting caught.

On his final lap, he knocked on Mrs. Bigelow's door and turned on his full Richard charm as he asked if she and her students had heard anything unusual, because he thought he had, but he couldn't be sure. Hands shot up as Mrs. Bigelow's current crop of experts in *Looking!* and *Listening!* confirmed that, in fact, *they* had heard the ringing of bells, not more than a few moments ago. Some were even pretty sure they had also caught a quick glimpse of tails flashing by the window, probably those of reindeer. There might even have been the sound of footsteps on the roof.

That was Richard's cue to present Mrs. Bigelow with a big pile of frosty ice blue letters wrapped in a red satin bow with the tiniest of icicles formed on the borders. "I found these outside your door and I wonder what they are. I guess it's *possible* that whoever was jingling those bells left these. Anyway, I think we'd better have a closer look."

Well, of course Mrs. Bigelow, the blackbelt in getting children of all ages to *Look!* and *Listen!* played her role wonderfully, telling Richard she would need some help making sure the letters got to the right people and could he think of anyone who could assist her young readers in making sense of all the words contained in the letters?

And that is how it came to pass, on this last hour of the Friday before Christmas break commenced, that thirty-one willing helpers from the eighth grade, waiting in the stairwell to Upstairs, where no kindergartners ever tread, suddenly materialized to read letters from Santa out loud to a gaggle of true believers.

In what could only be acknowledged as a Genuine Christmas Miracle, each teenager also had two cups of hot chocolate (with marshmallows!) and two gingerbread cookies that needed to be shared with someone. Did anybody in Mrs. Bigelow's room like hot chocolate and gingerbread cookies? They did.

And Richard, the least likely prophet in my small mind, led them.

There is no miracle God cannot work.

Check, Check, Check

Like good stewards of the manifold grace of God,
serve one another
with whatever gift each of you has received.

1 PETER 4:10

There's nothing quite like eighth-grade nostalgia, and I am not above harnessing it for my own purposes. With memories of *Operation Christmas Magic* still fresh in their hearts, my new eighth-grade authors meandered further down Memory Lane, this time recalling their favorite books from their first years in school.

I had just been to an in-service presentation about working with "disenchanted learners." The speaker had reminded me that *dis-enchanted* literally means "away from the magic." So, part of our charge as educators is to re-connect students with the stunning joy they once found in breaking open stories and mastering new skills in the "classics" they had read ages ago—as far back as six or seven years, or even longer.

Robert, who couldn't be bothered to crack to spine of *The Pearl* in our literature class, was, I found out, the same little boy who'd eagerly listened to *Ferdinand the Bull* so many times as a five-year-old that, I was told, long before he could read anything for himself he knew when his tired dad tried to skip a word to hasten bedtime. He *could* love stories, just not the ones I was foisting on him.

Julianne kept earning zeroes from me due to her inability to develop a retrievable homework filing system. But as a little girl she had spent hours seeking and finding that guy in the horn-rimmed glasses and red and white striped shirt, wearing out three different volumes in the *Where's Waldo?* series. She *could* focus. Just not on what I wanted her to.

Once upon a time, it seemed, every one of my eighth graders couldn't get enough of certain books. Finally, it dawned on me to quit fighting this and use it.

So I began encouraging my students to talk about the stories that had turned them from "decoders" into "readers." As they talked with one another, they got increasingly invested in the idea of helping their newly found kindergarten buddies fall in love with reading. And I began to realize that helping them do so might bring them back to the magic of learning they would need as they headed to high school and beyond.

First, they decided, they would like to read some of their own favorite stories out loud for the little ones. Copies of *Mike Mulligan's Steam Shovel, Where the Wild Things Are,* and *Madeline,* their duct-taped bindings bearing witness to how well-loved they'd been, trickled in from homes to our classroom, and a delegation was formed to meet with Mrs. Bigelow to see if she could possibly find thirty minutes one day to let the big kids pair up with the little ones to read aloud.

At the meeting, my students reminded the ever "skeptical" Mrs. Bigelow of what she had exhorted them to do all those years ago: *Look!* and *Listen!* And that is what they wanted to do with their "Reading Buddies," as they were now calling them, because they would be *Looking!*—paying close attention to the stories that made the kinders' eyes light up—and *Listening!*—trying to discern what this "younger generation" (truly my favorite term to come out of this endeavor) was thinking about. *They* had big plans for *them.*

The group finally prevailed on the wise Mrs. Bigelow to find thirty precious minutes a week for Reading Buddies. That is how one morning her classroom on the first floor became a controlled riot of gangly tweens who had even thought to bring in cushy pillows and blankets, the better to make Reading Forts with the buzzing kinders. The little ones could not believe that their heroes from the mysterious world of Upstairs were choosing to spend time with them again.

Mrs. Bigelow's reading loft groaned with all the pairs of students who wanted to curl up there for this event. She and I realized we would need to rotate people in and out so that they all got a chance in the prime reading real estate in their world. We loved the "problem" of eighth graders arguing over the best place to share a great story. Those who didn't make the initial loft cut were undeterred and told their charges they could make magic anywhere: That was the glory of books.

I had to marvel that these were the same students who mumbled their way through verbal proficiency exercises in my own reading class. But then, what did I know? I'm only a teacher.

Our first half hour evaporated, and on the way Upstairs my kids teemed with ideas. Next time just plain old reading out loud would not be good enough; now they would create sound effects and special voices and bring the stories their Buddies had told them they loved to uproarious life. And couldn't they "please, please, please, Miz Eifler," record them so that Mrs. Bigelow could use them later at her listening stations because "wouldn't it be a shame, Miz Eifler,"

to put in all this effort and have it disappear like dry ice at room temperature?

"Okay," I agreed with feigned reluctance, "but only on your own time."

"Yes, yes," they agreed too quickly. "At recess or after school when it's quiet in our room."

"It'll take some technology I don't have in the room right now," I pointed out.

"That's okay—we'll bring all the equipment from home." Some even offered to recruit their parents to help. Now I knew for certain that we were entering into uncharted waters.

My goal-oriented teacher mind hurtled through the proficiencies this little project was helping the students develop:

1. Persuasive prose? Check.
2. Productive oral language skills? Check.
3. Responsible collaboration? Check.
4. A few teetering steps back toward the magic? Check.

A Word We All Need

I have put my words in your mouth,
and hidden you in the shadow of my hand,
stretching out the heavens
and laying the foundations of the earth.

ISAIAH 51:16

This is a story about a word that doesn't actually exist, but should.

As we boarded a plane to Dallas for a teacher convention, one of my colleagues said, *sotto voce*, "Thanks for the gift of last night." The previous evening, I had insisted that James let me fill in for him at a parent-teacher conference while he spent some precious hours with his dying father and the rest of his family. If I'd been really ferocious, I would have persuaded him to stay home from Dallas altogether, but helping him carve out some time to fix the world's most comforting chicken and dumplings for his family and simply be present to his father for an evening was victory enough.

Perhaps my prodding James to that interaction with his dad would later allow me to experience a vicarious deathbed reconciliation of sorts with my own dying mother.

But my motivations don't really matter. What mattered was that James' dad felt the depth and breadth of his son's love for him, as did everyone else in his family, and that was the good thing.

En route to Dallas, James recorded the events of the previous evening, one of the last he would have with his father, in his computer journal. He privileged me with a reading of his account during a lull in the convention later that day. We both realized how fortunate we were to have stumbled into this affable teacher-to-teacher relationship in the middle of a frantic school year. Sharing laughter at inane moments of academic life, a zesty give and take while teaching the same students, friendly competitions to design the most outrageous bulletin boards and bring the best treats to faculty meetings, mutual respect for the spiritual life and a common gentleness of spirit—all these made us understand that our friendship was a fine thing, a delightful surprise for a couple of middle-aged teaching veterans. Like the saying goes, friendship isn't one big thing; it's a million little things.

What a blessing it is for teachers to have time to name and savor almost the whole million of those little things.

But here comes the birth of a new word, overlooked by me until my second or third reading of James' journal. I saw that his less-than-stellar typing skills had rendered the following: "Heartwrenchingly, I record this…with a god friend across the aisle." What he had intended to write obviously was "good friend," but "godfriend" captured our relationship perfectly. If the godfathers and godmothers chosen for us by our parents are to represent Christ's loving presence here on earth, it really seems as if there should also be a word to describe the people we ourselves recognize and collect deliberately along our own journeys who reveal astonishing aspects of God to us.

The question/answer sequence of the old Catholic catechism book I had learned as a child surged back in that moment, making perfect sense: "What is a sacrament?" "A sacrament is an outward sign, instituted by Christ, to bestow grace." James and I decided that *godfriend* encapsulates perfectly the grace-filled—and sometimes feisty—love, comfort, and peace that comprise the notion of sacramental friendship. He decided not to correct the error, and I concurred.

One month later, at another convention comprised of teachers from Catholic schools all over the country, Eva, a tremendous poet and one of the wisest women on the planet, was leading a discussion on the vocation of teaching. We were discussing our perceptions of God's place in our recent lives and work.

It had been a devastating year for me: my mom's unexpected death, upheavals at school, and the senseless murder of a former student with whom I was very close. I was feeling saturated and defined by these losses.

Seeking a moment of respite in the midst of this recent history, I eventually shared the genesis of "godfriend" with Eva, the wordsmith. She immediately worked the word into a poem-prayer, and several of our services during the week of workshops used it.

Our closing ceremony had each teacher present invoke the Lord's blessings on our "godfriends" as we sent one another forth to continue the ministry and vocation of teaching.

Not bad for a word whose life began as a typo.

The Communion of Saints

When he was at the table with them,
he took bread,
blessed and broke it,
and gave it to them.
Then their eyes were opened,
and they recognized him.

LUKE 24:30-31

Maybe it's the melamine trays and tiny milk cartons, but it's weird. One minute I am briskly, confidently managing a herd of unruly eighth graders down the hall to the cafeteria for lunch, making sure there are at least eight people between Richard and Amanda, aiming a wickedly effective Teacher Look at Jesse so he doesn't even *think* about tormenting Jessica, and making sure Julianne, our new girl, has someone to sit with.

The next minute, however, the crushable high school sophomore I once was, who somehow still lives within me, quakes at facing the tables of my teaching colleagues wolfing down their lunches in the twelve minutes they have until recess duty. They're all such nice people and have proven that to me time and again. Heck, I'm a nice person too. But there's something about carrying a food tray and hoping to be invited for a place at table that brings roaring back to life an insecurity in me that should have faded away a long time ago.

But here's another weird thing. At other times, a similarly unexpected flash of sensation brings back for a glimmer of a visit an earlier version of me that I've really missed. Like when I'm directing the students on the Social Committee to hold the cups sideways when they pour the root beers out for the class party and my Grandpa Quinn, buried these past forty years, taps me on the shoulder and says, "That's my girl; just like I told you." Suddenly I am my five-year-old self again as Grandpa shows me how to keep his Miller's beer from foaming over by tilting the glass as we pour.

Or a cursive "g" comes out especially lovely as I am writing out the day's homework tasks on the board and Sister Mary Therese Anne nods her approval at the ascenders and descenders she labored to help all fifty (fifty!) second graders in her care master during our Palmer Method handwriting lessons each afternoon at St. Joan of Arc School. Or putting down my Agatha Christie mystery on a blissfully booky rainy Saturday and momentarily feeling the room graced by Sister Mary Reynette, who helped me and forty-nine (forty-nine!) other first graders crack the code that turned squiggles into letters and letters into words. Or I am shaking hands with each of my students as they leave for the day, making sure that they have each heard themselves called by name and acknowledged by an adult. and my godfriend James, now deceased, is suddenly there on my shoulder, as his courtly gentleness is my inspiration for this ritual.

I love that even though my students will never know Grandpa or the good Sisters or James, they can feel their influence through the best of my actions as I channel what I learned from them and savor their occasional drive-bys into my consciousness.

I had a student once named Jaime who started wearing dress shoes to school each day, the kind with heels that clicked loudly every time he walked even the shortest of distances on our school's linoleum floors. And with the new shoes came increasing trips out of his desk: to sharpen his pencil (click, click), get his friends tissues (click, click), wander around looking at the walls (click, click), or ask if I needed anything taken to the office (about two hundred yards, roundtrip, of really loud clicking).

Jaime especially loved his trips alone down the school corridor, for the echo his shoes could produce in all that empty space. The rest of us did not see it that way, and it was not too long before Jaime's clicking made it hard for us to concentrate. It was time for a chat.

"Yes, I know these shoes make noise, Miz Eifler," he said. "That's why I bought them. On Saturdays when I was a real little boy, my father would take my mom for dinner and sometimes dancing. He would get all dressed up and put on his special 'going out shoes' and sometimes they would dance down our hallway and into the living room and his shoes clicked all the way on the hardwood floors. He and my mom looked so beautiful together as they swirled and clicked. I was four when Papa died of a heart attack. It's just my mom and my three brothers and me in the house now and nobody dances anymore. But when I wear these shoes, and they click, click, click down the hallway like his did, I always think of my father and he is here with me for a while, even though I can barely remember what he looked like."

Oh, God. Another teacher learning moment. Thank you, Jaime, for letting me know the communion of saints isn't just words in the last line of our creed but a lived reality. Those we loved and who loved us back return constantly to tap us on the shoulder and remind us we've got people in our corner. We wouldn't want it any other way, would we?

THOSE CRAZY PRESENT-TENSE BEATITUDES

Blessed are those who mourn,
for they will be comforted.

MATTHEW 5:4

One of the best things about teaching in a Catholic school is that when tragedies strike and we don't know what to say, we know exactly what to say. Like when our beloved music teacher Philip died.

The Beatitudes seemed an odd choice of funeral reading for Philip: "Blessed *are* the sorrowing; Blessed *are* the poor in spirit; Blessed *are* the meek." Christ's relentless use of the present tense was jarring. Tears and weakness are blessings? It made no sense.

Then they started the slideshow: Philip mugging for the camera as a youngster; Philip playing his ubiquitous trumpet. Philip wearing the thick toupee he wore for a while as he reinvented himself at one point, the one we pretended not to notice. Philip adoring each day allotted to him.

But the pictures of him when the tumor took its most vicious toll illuminated best how those who mourn could be blessed, and those who are poor in spirit could be too. It's not much of a stretch to show your blessed status when all is well. But when you are confined to a wheelchair and your head won't even support your toupee anymore and you are *still* able to marshal a luminous smile—well, in those last pictures, we who mourned caught a sacred glimpse of what is possible when the everyday defenses yield to what is always there waiting to be embraced.

Instances of apparent weaknesses giving way to graces that go unnoticed are actually not rare.

For example, autumn leaves in robust hues of sienna and vermilion are luscious. The crazy thing is, the pigments for that controlled riot of color are there all along. It's just that most of the year the chloroplasts (which make leaves green) shout and dominate... microscopically speaking. As fall rolls around, however, those colors subside and the others (which were always there) finally get their chance to shine. Those glorious hues are on the same leaves I barely give a thought to in their green form—it is the diminishing, the surrender, the hushing, that gives us a glimpse into potential. What a great lesson for teachers to remember. How blessed we are to be able to witness grandeur that is always harbored there in the cells of our students.

This brings Margaret powerfully to mind. Margaret exemplifies all the "gray children" who slip unheralded through classrooms. She never made trouble. She completed her work, but in unremarkable style. I don't remember her asking questions or raising her hand to offer anything. Until one day, when Margaret dazzled.

As the eighth graders filed in for math, there was an uneasy crackling of energy climaxing with two girls brawling. Juanita was one of them. Her opponent—and best friend—Teresa, ran out of the room sobbing furiously as Juanita retreated to her desk and collapsed.

Max related what had happened near the end of their previous class: Teresa had passed out notes to several people, taunting them to go back to Uganda...or China...or whatever country their parents had come from. When Juanita received hers, telling her to go back to Mexico, something had snapped and she had attacked Teresa in the hallway between periods. No one had a clue what had provoked the notes, but everyone seethed. The principal, Miss Wood, strode into the room, announcing that the two girls would be suspended for the rest of the week. They both gathered their things in sullen silence and left without a word. Miss Wood expected me to deal with the complicity of the entire class in the fighting.

As the class speculated about why Teresa had passed out the notes and why Juanita had reacted so violently, mousy little Margaret quietly offered the class her own thoughts. She had noticed a lot of bruises on both Juanita's and Teresa's arms and legs in the past few weeks. Maybe one or both of them were being physically abused at home.

"When you are being hit by the people who are supposed to take care of you," Margaret murmured, "you feel like lashing out at someone else. I know, because that is how it was for me a few years ago until my mom made my dad move out. I think Teresa and Juanita must be in a lot of pain to be taking it out on each other and the rest of us so badly. I think when they come back from suspension we should try to make them feel as safe and loved as we can at school, because it might be scary as hell for them at home. I know it was for me."

Every single person in the class could all hear the clock tick in the silence that met this searing, brave confession. Finally Derrick suggested a "Welcome Back" party for Juanita's and Teresa's return from suspension the next week. Assignments for food and drink were quickly negotiated.

The two girls returned to class the next week, their posture, gait, and downcast eyes telling us they expected a rocky re-entry. When they saw the "We Love You" banner and the treats gradually appearing, however, they both loosened up. Quiet, brave Margaret enveloped each of them in a hug, which they received haltingly at first and then collapsed into with clear relief.

The celebration that our class enjoyed that hour was not the usual eighth-grade raucous, but gentle and heartfelt. When Miss Wood asked later if I had come up with a consequence that would teach the class a lesson about the fight, I could truthfully assert, "Yes, they all learned something they will never forget."

Jesus was on to something when he used the startling present tense in each of his beatitudes. As we beheld Philip's resplendent smile on the screen, as Teresa and Juanita melted into the celebration engineered by their erstwhile friend Margaret, it made perfect sense to say, "Blessed are those who mourn." Not "will be," not "used to be, when everything ran along smoothly," but "are"—right now, in the heart of our fragility.

Asked and Half-Asked

I am about to do a new thing;
now it springs forth,
do you not perceive it?

ISAIAH 43:19

Trevor was trying to protect my delicate lady teacher ears and probably his own skin just a little when he told his group they shouldn't be doing such a "half-asked" job on their project. Everyone knew what he had started to say. But Trevor's inspired neologism stopped me in my tracks then and hovers years later. How often do we settle for a "half-asked" effort from our students? From ourselves? Even today, in the face of so-called "teacher-proof curricula" and public pressures to get students to perform well on high-stakes tests, it's not hard to tell the difference between teachers who make sure they engage every last bit of potential energy in their students and those for whom "half-asked" is the fool's gold standard.

Take my former colleagues Larry and Claire. They teach the same subjects to seventh graders, in classrooms across the hall from each other. Their students come from the same neighborhood and are randomly distributed between the two of them. They use the same textbooks; they adhere to the same curriculum framework—not that they have any choice in the matter.

Larry and Claire work on the same pay scale, started at exactly the same time, and have the same number of years until retirement. They are two sides of the same coin, joined at the hip, mirror images of one another, peas in a pod—in every way but their teaching.

Claireland is a joyous, vigorous place for kids to be, while Larryland is a pinched place for students and teacher alike.

Claire never gives less than all of herself to her students and encourages and catalyzes their own very best efforts from September to June. Her "Wall of Fame" outside her classroom features students' playful, insightful work. "Clever," her favorite compliment to pay them, doesn't come unless it is earned, making it quietly savored long after its bestowal.

In their annual study of *Alice in Wonderland*, Claire's students are known to cheer one another on with exuberant "O frabjous day, Callooh, Callay, we Chortle in our Joy!"

Larry, on the other hand, does the minimum he can get away with and not get fired. He can be found often checking his stock portfolio on his computer while his charges are burdened doing some sort of busy work. He posts anemic, if accurate, plot outlines by his students on the bulletin board outside his room. He passes out A's as if they were cotton candy—fluffy and unfilling—much to the delight of his students and their parents.

His favorite book is *The Legend of Sleepy Hollow*, delivered in a monotone without a bit of drama, which is mimicked by the children when they read aloud their own literary choices, which seem based primarily on the least number of pages they contain.

The difference between these two teachers is not a matter of form over substance; Claire's students know their stuff; Larry's go through the motions. A month after their simultaneously taught interdisciplinary unit on chocolate is in the grade books, Larry's students are pretty sure it might have had something to do with South America, while any one of Claire's students can tell you every country that produces chocolate, the status of their relationship to the U.S., how chocolate transforms from plant into a Snickers bar, and why it turns white after too much time in storage (but is still just fine to eat, which they will happily demonstrate for you).

At the front of Claire's room is posted a map produced by Ryan, a young man on the Asperger's Syndrome spectrum. It is a complex map that illustrates the path taken by the beans from one branch of a cacao tree all the way to a Hershey Bar at the local grocery store, accompanied by the math involved in every step of harvesting, production, and distribution.

What's really weird is that after years of working with her, Larry is always amazed at what even the lowest performing of Claire's students accomplish when they find themselves assigned to her classroom. The poor man actually thinks his colleague is annually "lucky" in the kids she draws, even though he participates in the selection.

The difference between them, of course, is talent and hard work. Claire's got it and does it, and Larry doesn't. There is a secret, however, that if Larry ever understood could go a long way toward making him more like Claire.

It's like the scene in the John Cusack movie *Say Anything*, where Cusack's character's high school friends are incredulous that he, a nondescript slacker, has gotten a date with the most gorgeous, gifted girl in the whole senior class. "How in the world did you possibly accomplish that?" they ask while hanging out in one of their teenage lairs. "You must be putting us on; there's absolutely no way that girl would agree to go out with you. What was your secret?"

"I asked her," he says.

Claire inspires. Claire ignites. Claire is a joy-bringer to formerly gray children, and she can be unsettling to those in Larry's universe who have always gotten by because they could go about things "half-asked."

Be Loved

Beloved,
I am writing you no new commandment,
but an old commandment
that you have had from the beginning.

1 JOHN 2:7

John, a fine writing teacher I knew once upon a time, grew to love what he called "inspired typos" even more than regular words—and this man cherished regular words. His favorite typos were those that eluded the Spell Check function on the computer, since they were merely existing words used incorrectly.

Sometimes these inspired typos were amusing, as when Jesse turned in a persuasive essay arguing that skateboards should definitely be allowed on the playground at recess. In the places where he had intended to write "definitely," however, Jesse had written "defiantly" instead.

This typo actually bolstered his argument in several places, or at least made it clear how strongly he cared about the topic: "I *defiantly* believe that boys would get in less trouble if they were allowed to use this device that means so much to them. We would *defiantly* be careful of the other students out there on the quad, and I can *defiantly* say that it would help burn off excess energy and help us concentrate better when we get back to class."

Jesse's essay won his class a two-week trial of skateboards at break-time from John. (The experiment was not a success, however, even though the essay was.)

51

Other times a typo illuminated for John a more searing truth than the desired word would have, as when Richard started an expository essay that was supposed to be about the "Lessons of History" but turned out to be about "Lesions of History" instead. People have certainly figured out plenty of ways to inflict cankers, scabs, and blisters upon one another in metaphorical and physical ways in our brief time on this planet, and Richard's typo opened a whole new way for his teacher to approach history lessons, starting with looking at the impacts of events on the lives of people, rather than as a string of names and dates.

With Richard's inspired typo in mind, John took the well-known photos of Little Rock Central High School from 1957, in which nine African American students are being escorted by National Guardsmen onto a campus viciously opposed to school integration, and posted them on a screen in his classroom. He also showed his students images of skin lesions and explained how those occur through chafing, scrapes, and burns. He then asked his students to consider the "lesions" that might be found in the hearts and minds of the bystanders in the Little Rock photo, who appear to be sneering and berating the young students, and in the minds and hearts of the young students, who themselves seem to be quaking on their relentless walk up the school stairs, clutching their books and maintaining an outrageous level of dignity in the face of the taunts and threats.

John asked his students to imagine what those white bystanders might think and feel today as they look back on their younger selves? How might the black students explain themselves to their own children when asked what was going through their heads in the photo? This would have been a solid lesson of history even if it had been taught the old way, but the *lesion* to be learned made it all the more unforgettable.

John's favorite typo of all time was Beth's series of quotations from the First Letter of St. John, who repeatedly—at least seven times in the first two chapters alone—refers to his ancient readers as "Beloved." Taken in that form, it is a perfectly uplifting message about walking in the light, forgiving one another's sins, loving rather than hating our brothers and sisters. But for some reason, each time Beth wrote the word, she rendered it as "Be loved," so it came across as a task, a charge, an imperative, rather than as a pet name.

The more John thought about this inspired typo, the more he was drawn to it. It captured what a daunting challenge it is for teachers to let ourselves embrace Divine Love that is freely given and always available. He started seeing so many opportunities in a teacher's life to "be loved": accepting compliments rather than deflecting them from students or parents when lessons soared; receiving a cup of coffee from a colleague who thinks we look tired and won't take a dollar in recompense; acknowledging at the end of a day that we really had done the best we were capable of doing, at least on that day.

Like an airline passenger following instructions to put on his own oxygen mask before attempting to help anyone else, John began the long discipline entailed by the simple command to "be loved."

He would be the first to recommend that path to other teachers. Defiantly.

Least Favorite Student

Truly I tell you,
just as you did it to one of the least of these
who are members of my family,
you did it to me.

MATTHEW 25:40

"What is the best true thing you can say about your least favorite student?" was the most haunting question Adrienne ever got asked in a job interview after she quit teaching high school. She gave it some thought.

There was her student Chris, who bugged her because he always knew more than anyone else in the classroom, including Adrienne herself. He was rarely diplomatic, but he was inevitably and maddeningly correct. Chris could always make the intuitive leap far beyond anything Adrienne was laying out, as if he were in her classroom but not quite of it. Adrienne came to imagine that the inside of Chris' brain was a drawing by M.C. Escher, you know, the one that has all the stairs going up and down but never ending anywhere.

Chris knew as much as he did because he devoured everything in print. During an ice storm that shut down their city and kept him from his precious public library, Chris found the owner's manual for his parents' Honda Civic, inhaled it, and remembered every detail. That is how relentlessly curious he was.

And as she contemplated her memories of Chris, Adrienne

realized that he was always, *always* able to articulate reasonable, imaginative answers to a frustrating pair of questions raised by his peers: "Why do we need to know this stuff?" and "How are we ever going to use it?" Where Adrienne sometimes defaulted to "for your SATs, that's why" or "it's in the mandated curriculum," Chris made elegant intellectual connections for his fellow students between mathematics and rap music, between literature and sports, between religion and the latest hit movie, and explained them in ways that made even Adrienne want to learn more. While she never quite overcame the shudder that accompanied seeing Chris' hand raised in her classroom, Adrienne could identify him as a person who found learning itself captivating, and that was an occasion of grace for her.

Andre came to mind too. Andre, who would not, *could* not, get to school on time and had to be brought up to speed every day on what he had missed those first thirty minutes. He was another frustrating one. At least he had the most charming smile Adrienne had ever encountered, she thought. But while that was true, it was not the best thing Adrienne could say about Andre. It had taken many long conversations with him during class, during lunch periods, and after school to piece together the best true thing she could say about the young man.

Andre did not get to school on time because he was essentially raising himself and his little sister. They had been deserted by a father who couldn't be bothered with the two kids he had sired and were ignored by a mother overwhelmed by the difficult life she had created for herself and her children.

Andre got himself to two jobs to make the family's rent. Adrienne knew about the first one, because she had encountered him often at her local supermarket and benefited from his careful bagging and cheerful help out to her car. She found out about the second one from one of her colleagues, who raved about Andre's courtesy and professionalism and, yes, his incredibly charming smile when he brought down her car one time close to midnight at the valet parking garage near the airport.

Putting these pieces together, Adrienne could truthfully say that Andre was the most resilient and self-reliant person she knew, even if he was always maddeningly late.

"That's a great question, and really tough to answer," Adrienne had to tell the interviewer. Not because she couldn't think of a straight, true affirmation to describe the students who'd contributed to her gray hairs. It was challenging because once she really started reflecting on her most challenging students, it was immensely difficult to select one that was truly her "least favorite."

When she really thought about them, her most trying students brought to life a line of her very favorite poem "As Kingfishers Catch Fire, Dragonflies Draw Flame" by Gerard Manley Hopkins:

> *....for Christ plays in ten thousand places,*
> *Lovely in limbs, and lovely in eyes not his*
> *To the Father through the features of men's faces.*

I Teach People, Not Geography

O Lord,
you will hear the desire of the meek;
you will strengthen their heart,
you will incline your ear.

PSALM 10:17

A hot Monday in late May. A portable classroom back in the days when Catholic schools were bulging at the seams. The windows wouldn't open, which was kind of an irrelevant fact in the middle of this third-degree smog alert in California's San Fernando Valley, when no one was supposed to be breathing anyway. An eighth-grade cocktail of fusty post-lunch sluggishness and eye-rolling boredom at the day's geography lesson on the great rivers of Europe. Not the conditions that bring out anybody's best. Certainly not mine.

Still, I was surprised and a little hurt when the sweetest girl in the class started chatting with her neighbor, as if my comments on the Danube flowing through four European capitals were trivial. Disciplinary salvo number one: "Mary Kate, you know better than that." And on we went to the Danube's source in the Black Forest of Germany, leading to more off-task murmurings from Mary Kate, sitting right there in the front row. Can't you see me, girl?

I tried an I-message: "I really need you to stop talking while I am teaching." Better for a while, as this girl never gets into trouble and is gratifyingly pink. But just as we were emptying the Danube into the Black Sea, I could not believe my eyes: Now she was passing a note.

"Mary Kate," I said, a little more shrilly than I intended, "you know the three-strikes-and-you-are-out rule we have in this classroom. You march yourself to Miss Wood's office and tell her you got yourself kicked out of class. I really don't know what got into you."

Mary Kate looked embarrassed. She should have; she had interrupted my lesson.

She shuffled out of the rank, airless portable classroom, where we had now moved on to the Rhine. Mary Kate was not looking forward to her first-ever visit to the principal's office. But geography was just sooooooo boring. Still, talking when the teacher is lecturing is rude, and she figured she deserved whatever punishment Miss Wood would hand out.

The secretary, Mrs. Conrad, told Mary Kate to have a seat, as Miss Wood was over at the rectory. Would Mary Kate like a Popsicle while she was waiting? The Popsicle was a nice surprise, but not nearly as nice as the astonishing realization that this office was nicely air-conditioned. It also didn't smell like thirty-five eighth graders after lunch recess on a smoggy day. It was quite quiet here on Miss Wood's comfy visitor's chair.

As it turned out, Miss Wood's meeting took the rest of the afternoon and the secretary got busy and forgot about Mary Kate, and so the girl was left alone all afternoon in the cool, still office, away from the hated river lecture.

How did this happen, she asked herself. A hypothesis formed, which she would test the very next day.

New hot day; new river. We were on the Elbe now, and I had barely gotten into its major tributaries (Saale, Havel, Mulde) when

Mary Kate started talking again. (Just one day after you've been to the principal's office for the first time? Really?) This was too much, and I banished her again after she used up her last two strikes even more quickly than she had done the day before. Her complicit friend Laurie got banished too. Mary Kate held her breath on their walk up to the principal's office to be punished; she didn't want to get Laurie's hopes up yet. But sure enough, Miss Wood was engaged with the PTO in the cafegymatorium and Mrs. Conrad told the girls to have a seat in her office and, by the way, would they like a Popsicle on this muggy day?

Unpunished by Miss Wood, whose PTO meeting took the rest of the afternoon, the two girls settled into the serene, air-conditioned splendor of the place and hatched a plan to aid their entire class.

The next day, we had not even learned our first fascinating fact about the River Seine when the class appeared possessed. Everyone was chattering with someone else, passing notes and ignoring the lesson I had so carefully crafted.

I snapped. I lost it. I sent them all up to be punished in the principal's office. I felt pretty silly, sitting in my classroom by myself, but by God I had to put my foot down. Didn't I?

Except that a few minutes later they were all being marched back into the classroom by Miss Wood herself, who finally had an open slot on her calendar to attend to the ruckus in my geography class. But it wasn't the students who got the lecture, it was their teacher. Miss Wood connected the dots for me about the psychological notion of "negative reinforcement," in which an organism will increase any behavior that removes an unpleasant stimulus. In textbooks, this concept is usually illustrated with lab rats learning to walk the one path that does not deliver an electric shock. Eighth graders are way more complex than rats, and droning lectures in stifling classrooms on smoggy afternoons are as undesirable to them as electric shocks are to rats. Kicking them out of that environment, not to mention plopping them into a cool, spacious office complete with Popsicles from our kind secretary, had not only *not* punished them, it had reinforced the very behaviors I meant to squash.

I am not the first or the last teacher to ignore what my students needed and forge ahead with a lesson that died as it was being delivered. But thanks to Mary Kate for reminding me that I teach people, not geography.

Plus, the rivers of Europe have just got to get more interesting.

PROBING THEIR WOUNDS

Put your finger here and see my hands.
Reach out your hand and put it in my side.
Do not doubt but believe.

JOHN 20:27

I don't have a lot of experience with physical wounds. My son never fell off his bicycle seriously enough to need more than sympathetic maternal murmurings. I have not had to deal at school with much beyond the occasional scraped knee or elbow I have tended during countless periods of recess duty. But some wounds are not inflicted on the body and are just as painful to children.

I think there is more to the story of Thomas, the Doubting Apostle, than an exhortation of him by Jesus to believe the unfathomable, even without tangible proof. What might it mean to take Thomas not as the antithesis of what we teachers need to strive for but as our role model for how to deal with the wounds of our students?

Thomas—quaking perhaps, but apparently voluntarily—was still willing to probe the gaping slash in Jesus' side. What if we look at him as an exemplar of empathy, literally one who *"feels with"* another? Surely that is part of what it means to "reach out your hand and put it in my side." Anyone with at least two minutes in the teaching profession has encountered enough of others' wounded spirits to fill a whole month of Mondays.

The fifth grade boys didn't really know what the words meant; they were just parroting what they had heard on their older siblings' music players. "Ho" (for "whore") was easy to spell and came out of the mouth with a satisfying punch. All these suburban Little Leaguers knew about the meaning of the slang word was that it was impolite, but really, how bad could two simple letters be? The perfect thing, a group of them decided, for tormenting Allie and Laura, the two smartest, hardest working students in their class. They were "hoes."

There were notes left in backpacks and quiet taunts on the playground. Allie and Laura started asking if they could stay in and clean up the classroom instead of going out to recess. Their hands didn't go up during discussions anymore. In a busy class of thirty-six, those little signs of something very wrong can escape a teacher's consciousness pretty easily. The nickel finally dropped for me when I was shepherding the line on the way down to the cafegymatorium for phys ed. At some invisible cue, all the boys—the same boys who always clammed up resolutely during music class—started singing "Hi ho, hi ho, it's off to work we go" in perfect unison and with suspicious gusto on the "ho." Tears that had been pent up for a couple weeks of covert verbal bullying finally flowed and the story tumbled out of the two girls.

For the class, probing the wounds started with being willing to listen to what the girls had been through. Allie and Laura hadn't really had anything but a glimmer of the word's meaning either when the torment started, but they were smart girls who could find and read online slang dictionaries. They were being called whores, prostitutes, call girls, sex workers.

The boys were shocked at what their classmates found out about them and embarrassed at having this conversation with their female teacher and having to look their victims in the eye to begin the long apology. To their credit, without protest they did an oral report for several other classes on the not-so-benign meanings of a lot of lyrics from popular songs.

Every day we teachers get a dozen or so such chances to embrace and thereby shore up the wounds students share with us. Let's be like Thomas and not be afraid to touch those wounds.

DIVINE Providence

IT All MATTERS

INtentionality

STUDENTS

TEACHERS

Graced ENcounters

Humility

NEVER KNOW what
is going on...

PICTURE DAY

There is a balm in Gilead,
to make the wounded whole.

TRADITIONAL SPIRITUAL

Sometimes teaching the "whole person" means teaching a "fractured person." We were talking about that the other day at school, and every teacher at the table had a story about gently putting wounded pieces back together, even if their Gilead was in an algebra or social studies classroom.

Tess Miller remembered Jim, a ninth grader she had in her homeroom and math classes a few years ago. His mom died from cancer right before school started. The mother had been a vibrant, helpful force at the school and an amazing parent to her four boys, of whom Jim was the oldest. Her death changed him for several months as he withdrew into some dark space in himself and rebuffed his old friends' attempts to draw him into the old activities he'd once enjoyed.

Symbolic of this change in Jim was the mohawk hairdo he adopted soon after the funeral. Using glue and water, he formed long sharp spikes of black hair from his forehead to his nape, with the hair on either side completely shaved off. The sharp points embodied the new prickliness of his personality.

As school picture day neared, Tess gently asked Jim if he wanted to make any changes to his hair. After all, pictures capture a moment forever. Maybe when he was looking back at the yearbook years from now, he might have a regret or two? In surly monosyllables, Jim assured his teacher that it was none of her business what he looked like and that he did not care at all what his school picture looked like. "So back off, will you?" he said fiercely.

And so the worst season of Jim's life was indeed captured and printed onto an 8 x 10 portrait and twenty-five wallet sized photos. And that was the photo that was to be used on the class sheet, with all the graduating students, their teachers, and the principal.

Even the worst seasons of grief eventually give way, if not to something better, at least to a reduction from steady throbbing pain to the occasional manageable ache. For Jim, the beginning of that relief was the Monday that the contact photos were delivered to homerooms and he got a look at the stark mohawk and icy glare staring back at him. He stormed up to Tess and demanded, "Why did you let me do that? My mom is going to kill me," before realizing what he had just said. And then the tears flowed, both Jim's and Tess', as he crumpled into her astonished arms and she could provide him the maternal embrace he'd been separated from for months.

"There is no way I can have this picture in the yearbook, Miz Miller. What about make-ups, like what if I'd been absent on picture day, can't we do something like that?" Jim started to wheedle, most of his defenses melting in the healing tears he was finally shedding. "Well," Tess countered, "you weren't absent that day and I did ask you if a mohawk was the way you wanted to go."

"And that is what is so cool, Miz M. That is exactly what my mom would say. You saw this was a stupid thing for me to do and you let me do it anyway after warning me. You didn't treat me like a leper. You've been like that this whole term, not cutting me slack just because my mom died. You even give me zeroes when I don't turn in my assignments. In a weird way, it's cool that I could fail your class this quarter, because that's normal and nothing has been normal for me since my mom got diagnosed. You totally keep your promises, even if you feel sorry for me. But now how are we going to fix this? I'll work my butt off, but I'm throwing myself at your mercy. This just cannot be my school picture, especially this year, and I don't want to flunk out of freshman math."

The solutions were simple and helped Jim start putting the pieces of his wounded spirit back together. He got double the homework in his math class and all the help he would ask for, the same treatment as Tess would have given anyone else in her class trying to bring a failing grade up to a passing one. As for the make-up pictures, which were supposed to be only for students absent on Picture Day, Tess wrote a note for Jim to give to the photographer on make-up day: "To Whom It May Concern: This brave and honest young man in front of you is one who was not present on the original Picture Day. I grant permission for you to let him sit for a make-up photo. Sincerely, Ms. Miller."

Over twenty years and a thousand students later, Tess still has one of Jim's twenty-five make-up wallet photos on the bulletin board behind her desk. Written in Jim's inimitable scrawl on the back: "Thanks for picking up the pieces, Miz Miller. The mohawk was a very bad idea. Love, Jim."

THE POWER OF THE PERSONAL

Jesus laid his hands on his eyes again;
and he looked intently
and his sight was restored,
and he saw everything clearly.

MARK 8:25

There were a lot of things Liz never expected to say as a teacher, and "I am not holding a conference with you about your son on your Blackberry" was one of them. With due respect for the important real estate deal Trevor's mom was trying to close, hence her breezy request for skipping the face-to-face meeting they had scheduled, Liz dug in and started reeling off (in her mind anyway) all the reasons meeting in person was essential when it came to parent-teacher conferences. When it came to just about any school interaction, for that matter. She dubbed this list "The Power of the Personal," and she revisits it at the beginning of every school year at her high school.

Ted was in her English class years ago and, truthfully, when he called to thank her for being the most important teacher in his life, the one who inspired him to earn a doctorate in English Literature, she had a hard time summoning a face to go with the name. But he made her cry when he told her he'd never forgotten the time she shushed everyone to hear his theory of why Iago was such a mean guy and looked him in the eye when he was done and said out loud to the whole class "Ted has a point there" and how in just five syllables she had transformed him into someone with a voice and ideas worth exploring.

To be honest, Liz could not recall that vignette three thousand students later, but she believed Ted when he told her it was catalytic for him. She knew that people can only feel truly seen when they are eyeball to eyeball with someone who matters to them. You can't look someone in the eye on a Blackberry, even if it has picture-in-picture technology.

Evil invaded Liz's school one awful day in the form of a lunatic who strangled a gentle young woman in one of the rooms, a dear heart who left a legacy of kindness. As the school lurched its way through the awful weeks after the crime, Liz had to bury her own grief to be strong for her students. (So decreed the memo from the principal.) One late Friday afternoon, however, her façade shattered and Liz let her tears of loss and fear and rage gush. She wasn't letting anyone down, she reasoned, since it was a Friday and she was alone in the elevator. Surely the universe could spare her stiff upper-lipping for thirty seconds.

Liz stepped out when the doors opened, still heaving pent-up sobs. "It's hard, isn't it?" came a soft voice in front of her. Katrina, a quiet student still at school for some reason, opened her arms and Liz fell into them and didn't care how hard or long she wept as one of her students held her and let her be. And somehow Katrina knew just when to let her pure embrace end and let Liz go back to work, restored. You simply cannot enfold a soul in pain on a Blackberry.

Fearless, warm-hearted Manny, whose signature on every single assignment he ever turned in was: "An Epic by Manny." At the height of the "Lord of the Dance" Irish step-dancing craze, Manny charmed a couple of classmates from semi-professional troupes into giving him lessons, and then he charmed Liz into letting him demonstrate what he'd learned to the class on an otherwise blah Thursday afternoon. Manny was all gawky legs and arms, not at all the kind of compact physique best suited for this highly controlled art form—more "Scarecrow" in *The Wizard of Oz* than Michael Flatley. But Manny filled the room in his kelly-green trousers and mango sweatshirt from the bargain bins he loved to haunt.

With sixteen-year-old chutzpah and flourish, Manny swept Liz into his dance, to the astonished, milk-coming-out-of-their-noses delight of the class. Her students were astounded at seeing their teacher work to catch her breath from the reeling and stomping of Manny's spirited, gangly version of Irish dance. None of that would've or could've happened on a Blackberry.

All these, and so many more, were graced moments of memory for Liz. Hauling her list out from time to time provided booster shots of zeal to fortify her for the face-to-face vocation she loved. And so, no, she would not hold a conference on a Blackberry.

WRITTEN ON THE HEART

I will put my law within them,
and I will write it on their hearts;
and I will be their God,
and they shall be my people.

JEREMIAH 31:33

Seven days ago, Rebecca had been the most popular girl in her class. Now no one would talk to her. Well, "popular" might be stretching it a little bit. Certainly her opinion seemed to matter the most to the other girls when they got new haircuts or wore new outfits to school. But earning a bored "cute" from her triggered not delight so much as relief at dodging her usual scathing "opinions." Two-year-olds are noted for playing *around* one another not *with* one another, and that same distinction described Rebecca's interactions with her peers. When people were assigned to be her partner, they got a bit breathless and stumbled over themselves to do most of the work for her, while she looked on from a regal, apparently disinterested distance.

Rebecca was part of a group (along with Julie, Samantha, and Kathy) that her teachers, in the sanctity of the faculty lounge, called the Gang of Four. The Gang of Four ruled the roost at the Catholic elementary school. There were rumors that each weekend they drew names of their classmates to torture via the silent treatment or noncommittal disapproval in the upcoming week, working their way through the entire class every six weeks or so.

By keeping their judging criteria completely to themselves, they elicited wild, desperate behaviors from many girls and just plain goofy behaviors from boys who were trying to please them or at least deflect their withering stares and scalding comments.

This center simply could not hold, especially in a system as volatile as middle-school social networks, and one day Rebecca found herself in violation of a mystery code concocted by the other Gang of Four members. Her history of minor cruelties to everyone else made her position especially precarious. On the one hand, her three "friends" scorned her and offered no explanations why or possible penance that might lift their scorn. On the other hand, since the list of people she'd shown genuine kindness to was incredibly brief, none of the other students owed Rebecca a place beside them at lunch or an invitation to study for the algebra test on Thursday. She had worked herself into a dark and lonely place indeed.

On the day Rebecca erupted into tears of frustration and rage that would not stop, even as all that salt threatened to swell her eyes shut, her religion teacher, Mr. Robinson, came to her rescue with a lesson she promised never to forget: He shared God's pledge from Jeremiah with her, where God promises to write the Law *on* people's hearts.

That's an odd preposition, *on*, the teacher pointed out to her. It would make more sense to write something as important as the Law *in* people's hearts, where it would be protected from falling off. "But I've been watching you this year, Rebecca, and this day has been coming for a long time. Would you agree you are about as low as it's possible to go? Can you imagine being any sadder? And isn't it wretched that you have made it nearly impossible for people outside of your three best friends to care about how you are doing?"

Rebecca admitted that she had really messed up.

"Here's the thing, Rebecca," Mr. Robinson told her. "God wants the Law, which is really all about love, to fill your heart, but only if you want that too. God doesn't want a relationship with a doll or a robot. That would be no better than those kids who were nice to you only because they wanted to be on your good side without really knowing you. Most of us are not going to turn to God until we are pretty desperate and have come to the limits of what the people around us can give us. I think you have finally figured out the limits of what Kathy and Samantha and Julie can offer you. God puts that Law *on* your heart rather than *in* it so that when your heart breaks, as it has been doing all week, all the love that is God's Law can come flooding in through the cracks and start tenderly putting the pieces back together."

Rebecca nodded. Not so much in understanding as in relief that someone was recognizing her grief.

"Heartbreak like you're feeling right now is an amazing opportunity for grace to turn things around for you, if you let it," the teacher explained. "That will take some work from you. I'll help you, if you're willing to try. Lucky for you there are plenty of heartbroken kids right here at this school who let God's love seep in through the cracks. Betcha they'll give you a chance if you make a sincere first move."

It was a long walk down the hallway Rebecca was used to owning. But some love, the real kind, that flows from one broken heart to another and starts to bind up old wounds, was on its way into her life.

On "Not Working"

*Those who are wise
shall shine like the brightness of the sky,
and those who lead many to righteousness,
like the stars forever and ever.*

DANIEL 12:3

My dad taught me an important lesson by accident the other afternoon. He phoned me at home and asked if I was busy. When I told him I was writing some lesson plans and organizing materials for the upcoming week, he said "Oh, good, I'm glad I caught you when you weren't working." It occurred to me that people who toil mightily in other fields, as my dad does, see the work of teachers much differently than folks who spend their days in the classroom trenches. For them, the work of teaching are those few hours a good teacher spends physically in a classroom, dispensing truth directly to students. That public aspect is surely part of any teacher's work, but so much goes on unseen to make those moments possible and fruitful.

Joan's students devour every word she says in her literature classes and dive into her assignments because of the hours she has invested sending personal notes to them during her travels: actual, authentic, handwritten postcards with stamps in an era of all-electronic, fill-in-the-variable-field communication. And all the parents of students in Joan's classes get at least one personal phone call during the year, informing them of something bold, productive, or creative their child has done. Since parents love it when their teenagers are caught in the act of doing something right (for a change), they tend to be fully on board with Joan's ambitious plans to turn each of her students into an accomplished reader and writer. So they provide her the kind of follow-through at home that most teachers can only fantasize about.

There are no cracks to fall through in Joan's classroom, because she creates and sustains a network of human relationships impenetrable to boredom, ennui, and anonymity. She has former students in every region of the country, and when one of her protégés is about to graduate and head off to college or the military or a job, Joan is able to connect them to fellow alums of the "Joan Treatment" via a personal letter of introduction, composed and mailed during some ten-minute stretch of "not working."

Then there is Stephanie, who moves her high school math students outside the familiar confines of Euclidian space by purchasing kale when she is "not working." It turns out that kale's ripples perfectly illustrate the leap from staid $y = mx + b$ graphing to a kind of algebra that a person would need four chalkboards of mostly incomprehensible squiggles to represent. Stephanie knows that she teaches students, not concepts, and that students, like the Doubting Apostle Thomas, are often more convinced of existing truths when they are literally invited to put their hands on them.

Stephanie gives all her students some kale to manipulate as she walks them into the mysterious new realms of advanced algebra and pre-calculus. And just as Thomas became one of the boldest of the apostles after his hands-on experience with the risen Christ, Stephanie's students fan out over the entire campus bringing the elegance and mysteries of modern math to the complacent and the confused.

I still reel from the demonstration of the existence of certain triangles that contain more (or less) than the one-hundred-eighty degrees of angles that I learned was Absolute Truth in my own high school math classes. And this from a shy student I could barely get to talk in my own class! But Stephanie unleashed this young woman's capacious and astonishing mind, turning her onto something nearly transcendent that the girl just had to communicate to her math-challenged literature teacher.

Rainer Maria Rilke's poem "The Swan" captures the industrious work of teachers "not working." Rilke describes how when walking, swans appear to be waddling clumsily, clearly laboring to get from one point to the next. But when a swan descends into a lake, it embodies graceful elegance. Or in Rilke's verse:

> *...letting himself fall*
>
> *into waters, which receive him gently*
> *and which, as though with reverence and joy,*
> *draw back past him in streams on either side....*

However, that is only what we see above the surface. For although the swan is gliding with no apparent effort expended, underneath the waters, his legs are roiling, paddling like crazy.

It only *looks* like he is not working.

Tell It Slant

*The child's father and mother were amazed
at what was being said about him.*

LUKE 2:33

Parents of "pistols"—students that are just too hot to handle—can have it tough at conference time. So often those "pistols" happen to be boys. By the time their son has gotten to high school, and probably much earlier, they have heard every teacher euphemism conceivable: "high-energy," "innnnteresting," "definitely has his own way of doing things." Roughly translated, those mean, respectively, "will not sit still no matter how many times I tell him," "undecipherable and nowhere near the assignment I actually gave him," and "unwilling to follow the simplest direction."

Chris' mom cracked open my heart on this way of dealing with irksome students one afternoon during one of those random encounters teachers have that change the way we look at some things.

Chris was definitely high energy, innnnteresting, and had his own way of doing things. He had a restless, seeking mind that devoured books, footnotes, and even nutrition labels on cereal boxes. Chris understood instinctively that the syllogisms and logic exercises he worked on in his geometry class made him write more effective expository essays in my English class. He correctly worked "adumbrate" into a casual class conversation one day. I know this, because I immediately looked the word up.

Chris was the kind of pistol who was usually assigned a position in the far outfield during phys ed class to accommodate his endless reveries. He was so voraciously inquisitive that, if we stumbled across something new or unknown to him, he'd immediately look it up—not just the meaning of whatever it was but the history, current status, and future implications of the entire subject.

We teachers say we treasure curiosity, and most of the time I think we mean it. But it can be hard on our ego to have a student know bookloads of facts beyond the day's lesson plans. I have to confess—to you, my brothers and sisters—that there were days I found myself hoping Chris came down with chicken pox or some such. Nothing serious or health threatening, mind you, just enough to keep him out of school for a few days while I caught my breath. Chris, of course, had perfect attendance.

All this ran through my mind in a few microseconds of neuro-processing when I literally ran into Chris' mom in the school office one afternoon. I was so deep in my own thoughts that I greeted her with the lamest of all teacher greetings: "Oh, you're Chris' mom, aren't you?"

The mother's look was so apprehensive that I feared I had dislocated her shoulder or crushed her foot in our collision. "Oh no," she groaned, "what has he done this time?"

For just as speedily as I could list all the ways Chris wore me out, it turns out his mom could recollect the dozens of parent-teacher conferences gone badly over the years, all the times teachers had launched into a list of what was wrong with her precocious son. And this is how I know there is a Holy Spirit who breathes life and love and wisdom into us teachers, just when we need it. I looked Chris' mom in those desperate eyes of hers and heard these true words come out of my mouth: "You are raising a young man with an amazing mind that astonishes me every day with its agility and boundless energy. And you must have done something we should all bottle and drink greedily from in the way you taught him to revere learning and books and never to settle for easy answers. What a gift you are sharing with the world."

To this the mother answered in a whisper, "Thank you so much, Miss Eifler. Do you know that this is the first time in ten years of schooling that a teacher ever started a conversation by telling me something nice about my son? I am never going to forget this. Thank you." And then she gave me a Mama Bear hug that squeezed forever into me this message: Every student in my classroom, even the "pistols," is someone's cherished son or daughter.

"Tell all the Truth," as Emily Dickinson wrote, "but tell it slant." We teachers need to start every conversation we have with parents by acknowledging the love they lavish upon their "pistol" children. There is no other way that they will hear us or listen to what we say.

The Tongue of a Teacher

The Lord God has given me the tongue of a teacher,
that I may know how to sustain the weary with a word.
Morning by morning he wakens—
wakens my ear to listen as those who are taught.

ISAIAH 50:4

My husband, Mark, and I are Lamaze-class dropouts. We grimaced, but stuck it out when the well-meaning instructor had everyone rub the pregnant bellies of the women in the room to acknowledge the presence of fifteen yet-to-be-born children. We endured the chenille peas and carrots she passed around to give us all hands-on experiences with healthy eating habits.

But she lost us when one of the women asked about epidurals and inquired when in the birth process we could ask for one. "Well, the whole point of this class is to avoid asking for drugs," the facilitator countered. "After all, women have been having babies for thousands of years without them."

"Yes, but if we need one, when do we get it?" I asked.

"Honestly, I promise that if you follow the procedures you are learning in this class, you won't need any drugs *and* you will get this wonderful baby out if it *and* you will be in a much better condition to respond to your child immediately after the birth."

I had no doubt our Lamaze instructor truly believed what she was saying, and Lamaze *is* supposed to be about natural childbirth. But she fully lost Mark and me when she finally asserted, "Of course there is the *occasional* woman who experiences *some* discomfort during childbirth."

We picked up our mat and never looked back. Twenty-two years later, I still send my anesthesiologist Christmas cards.

I was thinking about this story the other day and reflecting that teachers are a tough crowd for other teachers. I probably would have found *Ms. Au Natural* a little silly no matter what my profession, but as a fellow teacher I was also embarrassed at the lessons she had prepared and how she handled this group of adults. None of us had to be there, and I know we were all desperate for reliable, trustworthy instruction in the most profound task we would ever undertake. How many teachers yearn for a roomful of highly motivated, engaged learners with perfect attendance and a deep desire to succeed in the subject matter?

This woman had thirty of us right there and drove most of us away by the end of the second session.

Over the years, I've attended, voluntarily and otherwise, countless in-service presentations aimed at making every teacher there better at what they do, regardless of their classroom contexts or the makeup of all the worthy souls they attend to each day. Music and phys ed teachers sit through "Math across the Curriculum" sessions (although math teachers, interestingly enough, are rarely asked to attend sessions aimed at improving the teaching of music or PE).

But right up there with mind-numbing props such as the Lamaze stuffed peas and carrots are in-service instructors who lecture on things like the perils and limitations of lecturing. Lately, of course, these presentations have been fleshed out with PowerPoint slides slathered in tiny text that are nothing but walls of words.

My favorite example of this kind of waste of teachers' time was a gathering of nearly six hundred of us in a cavernous space, having to spend five hours listening to someone talk about "differentiated learning," which is just Edspeak for a teacher's need to meet the multiple and individual needs of his or her varied learners. There was no time for asking questions in that session; the presenter was on a tight schedule to cover a vast amount of material. But one of her key points was the importance of us ensuring that all of our students have ample opportunities to pose their individual questions. Uh-huh.

We teachers have always imparted facts, lots of them, to our students, and most of us are on fire to do that impeccably well. Those of us who have been in a classroom for about eight minutes or so also know that we must counsel, mend, coach, exhort, chastise, and—at least in Catholic schools—make God known and loved to an endless stream of students vastly different from one another and mostly not sharing many of our own experiences. Teaching is joyful, maddening, exhilarating, frustrating work we all wish we could do better.

As I have been given the opportunity to work with teachers on their professional development, I've learned that one of the most startling, invigorating starting points is to have them tell me what they already know and do. I was inspired by Dr. Spock (the baby guy, not the *Star Trek* Vulcan), whose very first sentence in his most important book on how to raise children is: "You know more than you think you do."

Now, Dr. Spock did not let his readers stop with what they already knew, but he did dignify their experience and build from there. That is why I encourage all who teach teachers (and expectant parents, for that matter) to take the prophet Isaiah's words, *"The Lord GOD has given me the tongue of a teacher, that I may know how to sustain the weary with a word,"* as their mantra.

Few invitations are more rousing than "talk about one of your recent successes." The "tongue of the teacher" will be absolutely crucial in helping others figure out and understand their own strengths and weaknesses, victories and defeats.

It sure beats "Well, there is the occasional loser who experiences some problems...."

WEAVING CROWNS OF VERBAL THORNS

*And the soldiers wove a crown of thorns
and put it on his head,
and they dressed him in a purple robe.*

JOHN 19:2

The spiked brambles woven into a crown of thorns are a haunting element in the story of Jesus' passion. From cacti in deserts to humble blackberry bushes, even a single thorn prick can sear tender skin.

The soldiers must have experienced some pain themselves in crafting that crown. The act of weaving is not a hasty process, but deliberate and methodical, and it is impossible to handle thorns without piercing one's own fingers. My mind wanders to the image of a soldier, egged on by his colleagues, creating a crown from the branches gathered by the group as the cruel idea took place among them. Perhaps he was the youngest and needed to prove himself. Or was he a fringe member of the squad, seeking acceptance by carrying out this small act of barbarity? Or the clown of the group, making monstrous fun with the outrageous notion that this humble one could be the King of the Jews? Any teacher can relate to each of those possibilities.

As a veteran of countless recess and lunch duties, I have watched lonely children latch onto the smallest difference in a new kid to elevate themselves in the eyes of their peers. I remember Alex, who was the smallest boy in his class, with mild learning disabilities. In a small school, this meant everyone knew Alex's limitations well enough to keep the taunts of "pipsqueak" and "retard" alive and well for most of his career at the school.

Then one day, Paulo moved into Alex's class, fresh from Nicaragua, and speaking no English. Rather than seize this opportunity to form a new friendship with a fellow outsider, Alex led the way in ridiculing Paulo, from his pronunciation of English words to his lack of familiarity with the regular playground pursuits of the other boys. Alex seemed to forget that his cohorts were the very boys who regularly made his life miserable; he clung instead to whatever favor he thought he was currying with the in-crowd as he hurled his barbs at Paulo.

Sadly for Alex, his respite from adolescent social hell hardly lasted long enough to savor. When spring soccer season rolled around, Paulo, who lived and breathed the sport, became playground royalty—not only with the boys, who admired his skill, but also with the blossoming girls, who suddenly found Paulo and his accent exotic and attractive.

Such memories yield fresh insight. The Roman soldiers who wove the crown of thorns and pressed it onto Jesus' head surely had to wipe their own blood from their hands after the deed. They knew better than anyone the long road from Pilate's porch to Golgotha. They knew any man would stumble, crushed by the weight of the beam, and they were determined that the crown stay put. The only way that could happen was to push down hard. And those who push down hard on something made out of thorns are going to puncture their own skin. The soldiers may have carried the physical scars of their own act of barbarity for years. Deliberate cruelty to others doesn't just diminish us; it inflicts some of the same pain on ourselves.

Minds create the sarcasm that drips like blood into so many adolescent interactions. I use that image of blood deliberately here. Blood lingers; it's one of the toughest stains to clean. We speak of words "cutting us like a knife." It is one thing to cultivate nimbleness with language and quite another to cultivate that facility in order to wound another person.

Say something often enough and it becomes reality; or as one of my heroes, Elie Wiesel, states: "We are our words."

"Inverted Jenny" Students

*The stone that the builders rejected
has become the chief cornerstone.*

PSALM 118:22

A stamp recently sold to a Wall Street investor for $825,000. In 1918, someone mailing a letter bought it from the post office for its face value of twenty-four cents. It's not being nearly one hundred years old that makes this one-inch by one-inch bit of paper so valuable. Instead, it has been prized for decades because it is flawed. When it was first printed, one of the craftsmen accidentally put the plate holding the engraving of the "Jenny" bi-plane in the machine upside down, and the mistake was not caught until several pages of stamps had entered the market. The so-called "Inverted Jenny" stamp is one of the more famous postal printing errors. Other mistakes include skewed or missing perforations, misspellings, and incorrect paper stock.

These are all cosmetic errors due to carelessness, every single one of them, and yet their existence makes these tiny stamps highly prized by discerning collectors, far more so than their perfectly formed counterparts.

What would it be like if human imperfections improved our value, rather than lessened it? Perhaps one gift of sublimely talented teachers is to look at their students' flaws and see the face of God and Love it, with a capital L.

Take Leo. He has taught English and speech for decades to

squirmy adolescents. He's never missed a chance to notice a gangly boy being courtly or an acne-prone girl being lovely and to call them on it, suspending their teen purgatory for a blessed while.

When Kaitlyn thought having a stutter meant she could not recite her poem for the class for her first public speaking assignment, Leo assented to her recording it alone in the classroom after school. The next day, however, Leo and Kaitlyn played the tape for the class, who were astonished not only that it was Kaitlyn's assured voice coming out of the speakers but also that she could marshal such different voices to communicate the various moods of each stanza of the poem she read, "The Road Less Travelled."

Leo then seized upon the idea of recording other assignments from the "Inverted Jennies" of his classes, learning how to add music and sound effects to create intriguing soundtracks for their poems, short stories, and persuasive speeches, creating multi-media presentations long before that was a *de rigour* teaching technique.

Today Leo owns a groaning board of robust, nuanced, and unforgettable (he still shivers at one student's rendition of "Invictus") language celebrations that started with a stutter.

Leo also helped turn Robert into a legend among his peers after languishing at the bottom of the class food chain. Robert had been adopted at six days old after his birth mother signed away her rights to him in order to face her own demons. One of her legacies to Robert was fetal alcohol syndrome, which left him with extremely compromised small muscle motor skills. The boy had never been able to use a pen legibly and, as a consequence, hated writing. Effort was not the issue, nor was motivation; his body was simply not up to the task. For Robert, appearing defiant was far preferable to appearing inept, and so he usually did not turn in writing assignments, which naturally made his grades plummet.

But like all good teachers, Leo was a digger, and he found many times to talk with Robert. He found out that Robert had a great sense of humor, plenty of fascinating opinions, and often the facts to back them up. Robert had plenty to say and was pretty good at saying it out loud, but his flawed body turned those eloquent thoughts into indecipherable glyphs. Leo scrounged up a keyboard and helped Robert find an online touch-typing program that he could practice at home and in spare time during class. Both of them marveled as Robert's tangled, tortured pen-and-paper essays gave way to polished pieces. The quality of what was printed on the paper caught up with the articulate thoughts in Robert's head. The kid was *smart*.

And Robert was *fast*. He could type as fast as he thought, as fast as Leo talked, as fast as any classroom discussion could fly. Robert's classmates were dazzled. They tested his new skill by having him transcribe songs as they were being played; Robert crushed those. Such things were merely fun diversions though. What made Robert love Leo forever was that his teacher had looked upon a suffering student and helped him cultivate something he was better at than anyone else in the room, a capacity that might have remained hidden and left him languishing had Leo not honed in on an imperfection that proved a catalyst for transformation.

Leave the stamps to mere Wall Street investors.
Teachers like Leo know priceless when they see it.

Getting It Righter

A sower went out to sow his seed;
and as he sowed,
some fell on the path and was trampled on,
and the birds of the air ate it up.
Some fell on the rock;
and as it grew up, it withered for lack of moisture.
Some fell among thorns,
and the thorns grew with it and choked it.
Some fell into good soil,
and when it grew,
it produced a hundredfold.

LUKE 8:5-8

My friend Ellie pulled the first dandelions from her front yard last week. I am no gardener, but learned a lot from Ellie as we talked about taking a closer look at the pernicious weed that consumes so much of her scant gardening time. Both of us were struck by a number of lessons dandelions offer teachers.

When observed closely, the delicate fuzz on a dandelion is actually a cloud of minute barbs. When a frenzy of those spikes are dispersed to the wind, whether by a child's blowing, a gentle breeze, or even an accidental kick, they allow the fuzz containing the promise of more dandelions to anchor just about anywhere. Wouldn't it be great if we could develop so many "hooks" in our work with students that memories of the content we explore extended beyond their latest test? Those hooks could be vignettes and pictures and videoclips that illustrate key principles in the form of stories that engage more of our students' brains (therefore taking firmer root) than mere recitations of facts.

We teachers could work more diligently to get students to create their own hooks every so often, inviting them to create quickwrites, make movies, find metaphors, and point to sensory images to elaborate on challenging material.

It's hard to predict where dandelion fuzz will land, and we teachers can extend that metaphor into our teaching by creating multiple entry points into more lessons, especially the ones we really want our students to remember.

Dandelions are opportunistic and will grow wherever there is the smallest opening. They apparently care little about the soil composition, aesthetics of their spore's landing place, or whether it has southern or northern exposure. They look for a tiny fissure and occupy it.

What kind of learning would my students experience if I seized on openings in their minds and hearts with anything like a dandelion's tenacity? Maybe I need to spend more time talking with my students in those minutes before and after class, or invite email dialogues about themselves as learners to find out what captures their imagination and passion. Even if I am not able to work those interests into teaching the material, perhaps my students will perceive how invested I am in their mastery of the subject and formation as human beings. There is a saying that "students will not care how much you know until they know how much you care." Seeking those openings where students are potentially more receptive is one way to exemplify the care I wish to communicate.

Truth be told, I love the vibrant yellow of dandelions. Ellie does too. When it feels impossible to conquer the waves of saffron invaders, we can talk ourselves into seeing them as flowers, not weeds. Maybe some of the students who drive me craziest with their unwillingness to acquiesce to my particular vision of how learning should transpire need to be contemplated with similarly changed ways of seeing. Every now and again, when I have worked hard to present the Revealed Truth in a lesson as it came to me, a student responds with a pithier, more straightforward rendering that captures the thought more accessibly and memorably for everyone in the room. It may be worthwhile for me to re-frame the way I respond to those students and celebrate what philosopher Maxine Greene has called "the disruptions of the taken-for-granted," rather than grinding my teeth as I usually do. An even more radical notion: Perhaps this could happen at faculty meetings as well!

Despite being subjected to the same environmental conditions, and squirted with the outright hostility of chemical deterrents, the foliage on the dandelion maintains its robust green hue even as the grass around it withers to the color and texture of straw. That capacity hints at deep, efficient reserves of energy and mechanisms of resiliency that I could do well to emulate myself and nurture in my students and fellow teachers.

Ellie gets a fresh chance every spring to start over in her lawn and garden, and each spring she pledges, "This year will be different. I will treat the yard earlier, tend it more carefully, and surely face fewer undesirable results." Teachers say approximately the same thing each September: "I will do what I learned in that workshop, organize better, find out more about the students, pray for them, give them more and earlier feedback, and be less frazzled at the semester's end."

The list goes on. One wonderful truth worth celebrating about teaching, unlike many other professions, is that we do get a lot of fresh starts. Every time we begin a new unit or close out a grading period is an invitation to get it righter than we did the last time.

HOPING BOLDLY

Since, then, we have such a hope,
we act with great boldness.

2 CORINTHIANS 3:12

SPANISH: *Esperanza*
FRENCH: *Espoir*
RUSSIAN: *Nadezhda*
VIETNAMESE: *Hy Vông*

EMILY DICKINSON:

The thing with feathers that perches in the soul.

I like to keep learning more ways to say the word *hope*, because the quest keeps the concept in my consciousness. My students have all learned how to spot the "right" answers on many of my multiple-choice exams: They always pick the option containing a character whose name means "hope," because that is ultimately what I think the vocation of teaching is all about. I love that they have cracked that secret. I especially love it when they share their own stories about teachers who helped them learn how to hope, even when those lessons were disguised as civics or calculus.

Charles was the brightest, most charismatic student in Michelle's high school universe, and he was also the one who routinely frazzled the end of her rope. That is, when he even bothered to show up in class. Passionate about politics, Charles often cut school to work on voting drives and attended a daunting array of meetings of the local African American community. When he did make it to her U.S. Government class, he dazzled his peers and Michelle with his articulate, well-supported viewpoints on more issues than she herself had ever considered. And yet he was always on the verge of failing, due to his failure to turn in his work.

Other teachers let Charles pass with "courtesy C's," wagering that his community activism proved he had good academic skills. Michelle, however, had higher hopes for him and determined to prove he could be a good student. She cleared her evening calendar and showed up on time to three of his community meetings in a row, plopping herself right beside him to drop off the assignments he had failed to pick up in his most recent absences. Speaking with the boldness of true hope, she launched into him.

"No work in my class—and I mean the work I assign, not the work you are doing here, Charles—no pass," she told him. "Period. I am not debating this with you. You want to be the man who brings about meaningful change in your community, great. If there is such a person, I truly believe you are he. But you earn your office, your power, your position by paying your dues and making sure you are the best thinker, writer, speaker, and reader you can be. And you prove that by doing the work."

"Charles," she continued, "you can do that all the way to a full scholarship to any university; that is how good you can be. Right now you are a truant, just this side of a dropout, and we both deserve better. So do the people whose lives you want to change. What's it going to be?"

When Charles replayed that conversation for me later, it was after he had attended Michelle's class for two straight weeks and turned in every last bit of homework for the semester, a lifetime record for him. Where did this transformation come from, I needed to know. "Well, you just do not mess around with a lady who hopes her fingertips to the bone," he said.

What can you say to that except "Amen" and "Alleluia"?

Teaching is not for the faint of heart. Nor is it for the faint of hope. It is the audacity to keep coming back to a classroom full of hormonally revved teens whose heavily lidded eyes and sunken posture practically scream, "I *dare* you to care enough to keep trying to teach me." Or to teach in a room in which half the children leave for weeks at a time to accompany their parents whose work is transient and seasonal and precarious. It is the ability to hold fast to the conviction that we *can* inject a dose of grace into the world these worthy young souls inhabit.

That is hope, and hope is any teacher's wellspring. Call it *toivo* (Finnish), call it *höffnung* (German), call it *nozomu* (Japanese): Those who teach, hope.

Waging Peace One Email at a Time

Blessed are the peacemakers,
for they will be called children of God.

MATTHEW 5:9

Just when I am ready to chuck my relationship-bludgeoning computer for some carrier pigeons, a story like this shows up from one of my all-time favorite students, who is now a teacher himself. Via email, naturally.

Where most people would say, "I teach social studies" or "I'm a religion teacher," Tim is one of those teachers who honestly and guilelessly says, "I teach students" when asked what he does for a living. He does not realize that he changes the very air when he walks into a room, that people are drawn to his ability to reflect what it must be like to dwell in the presence of God. He is a holy, humble man who had a lot of great years left in him when he retired from his first career as a banker and earned a teaching degree—the same year he got his AARP card.

Tim wanted specifically to teach students who would not have access to extras such as music and art and languages. His music, just his voice and a single acoustic guitar, can fill a cavernous parish hall, and there is not a teachable concept he has not set to music, which is where we enter this story and why I am going to give my computer one more chance.

Tim currently teaches Spanish (*to students*, he would hasten to add) in the middle of Nebraska, and he composes music to help them remember colors and numbers and verb conjugations. In the old days, it would have been admirable enough for some two hundred students to move through his classroom each year, unable to get his tunes—and therefore the concepts associated with those tunes—out of their heads. But the internet has made it possible for this unassuming guy in a renovated farmhouse in Nebraska to create a recording studio and post his Songs for Learning Spanish to anyone Out There with a decent search engine who might need some next week.

One Friday evening not too long ago, Tim received an email from young Hediyah in Tehran, Iran, who had just graduated from the university there and was about to start her very first year of teaching Spanish. Like most brand-new teachers, once the thrill of signing her first contract had worn off, she was in a frenzy of rounding up robust materials. Just before the first day of school, Tim's site showed up in her online search. It teemed with just the kind of songs she had been seeking, but for some reason, nothing would download on her computer. She hit the "Contact Tim Himself Now" button to explain her dilemma.

Now a key set of details to keep in mind is that this young lady's first language is Farsi, of which Tim speaks zero words, matching her total of English vocabulary. And Tim will be the first to admit that, while he can teach clothing, colors and how to order from a menu in basic Spanish to Nebraskan children, he is far from fluent. So this entire exchange is occurring in Spanish, with Tim at the end of his day and Hediyah at the beginning of hers.

Could Tim help her? Well of course his generous heart went into overdrive and he spent a painstaking hour composing a perfectly conjugated message back to Hediyah, pledging to mail her a complete CD of all his Spanish songs, guitar chords, lyrics, and overhead transparencies to use in her classroom. Within a few minutes, Hediyah lofted back a response thanking Tim for his generous offer and contributions to a lasting peace, but surface mail would take weeks and, um, she needed the songs by Monday or so and, um, did Tim have an alternative way to get her the materials, say something from the twenty-first century?

Even though both teachers were reading and writing in a second language, Tim and Hediyah saw the humor and the power of their exchange. Tim got his teenage daughter to help him and within another few minutes, the original computer files were soaring through cyber space from Tim's computer to Hediyah's.

And so it came to pass that on the very next Monday, twenty-five children at a Muslim school in Tehran were singing the very same songs as a roomful of students at a Catholic school in Omaha on the other side of the planet, under the watchful eyes of their gentle, imaginative teachers who were using their computers to wage peace, one email at a time.

GOOD SAMARITANS

A Samaritan while traveling came near him...
and when he saw him, he was moved with pity.

LUKE 10: 30, 33

Teachers at a Catholic high school were sitting around the faculty lounge over triple-shot Tuesday lattes not too long ago, wondering aloud how certain students had turned out years after what was, to each teacher's mind anyway, a powerful lesson they had taught once upon a time.

Maggie described Brendan, probably the most materially spoiled freshman she had ever known. His dad replaced expensive history textbooks as quickly as Brendan lost them. It wasn't unusual for his dad's secretary to deliver lunch to Brendan, fresh from a local restaurant. Maggie related the time she'd been teaching a unit on Westward Expansion to Brendan's class and relating how the U.S. government often reneged on land treaties with Native Americans, occupying territory that had been promised in writing to various tribes. Most of the class was aghast at the inherent injustice of those actions and wondered how it had been possible to break such clear promises with impunity. Brendan offered another perspective. "Hey, somebody bigger and stronger needed the land more, so they took it. That's the way things work in the real world. Deal with it."

No matter what points his classmates raised in the discussion that ensued, Brendan countered with the same argument (that he had obviously heard at home): "Someone bigger and stronger needed it more."

Things got pretty testy that period. As the students trickled out to lunch, Maggie got an idea that was either brilliant or professionally self-maiming. Years later, as she told her colleagues about it, she was still not sure which.

Maggie took all Brendan's things out of his desk and laid them in a pile at his spot in the row. She then took the desk to an adjacent classroom and left it there. When Brendan and his classmates returned to finish the block period after lunch, Brendan asked what happened to his desk. Maggie told him "It's crowded at this school and someone bigger needed a desk, so I gave him yours." Predictably, Brendan claimed how unfair that was, and to each protestation, Maggie replied calmly "Someone bigger needed it more. Now sit down." Brendan played along for the rest of the period, rolling his eyes only a few times. No one in class argued on his behalf.

However, Brendan was surprised still to be missing his desk the following day and the next, a Friday. As Maggie was preparing to leave her classroom for the weekend, she caught sight of Brendan and his dad striding across the parking lot in a pretty determined manner. Uh-oh.

Before Maggie could say anything, the father said, "Brendan told me what you did to him this week, making him go without a desk."

"Yes, well, I can explain," Maggie began, but she could not complete the thought as the father, clearly a man used to controlling negotiations, barreled on, "I think that is brilliant! You should keep his desk in storage for the rest of the year. In fact, if you want, I can take away his bed at home and make him sleep on the floor. I will not have my son thinking it is okay for people to break their promises just because they are bigger than other people, and I pledge to you right now I will reinforce the stuffing out of what you are trying to teach him with this lesson. You have my backing one hundred percent. You are one gutsy lady!"

And so it was that Brendan went without a desk for a couple of weeks to help him understand the issue from the other side, making a theoretical concept as concrete as sitting on a linoleum floor trying to conduct academic business.

As Maggie shared that vignette with her colleagues, she wondered what happened to Brendan as he became a man. Did he honor his promises? Was he generous? Did he still think, deep down, that bigger people who want things are entitled to take them from weaker, smaller people? There is no way to know, and every teacher sitting with her had a satchel full of similar "I wonder what happened to" ponderings.

In the story of the Good Samaritan, one thing that never gets mentioned is that, as far as we know, the man who got beaten and left for dead on the road to Jericho never said thanks to the fellow who got him bandaged up, fed him, and arranged for his after-care. In a lot of ways, that makes this parable a perfect one for teachers, because we rarely get to see how the stories of our students end as we send them into the world. Despite that, it is hard to think of a teacher who doesn't labor to keep giving his or her very best.

Being moved with compassion will do that to a person.

The Grace of Vulnerability

*The last will be first,
and the first will be last.*

MATTHEW 20:16

"Please lend your lesson plan book to Fran so she can see how it should be done" read the note I got from my busy principal after the weekly check she made of all our lesson plans. I knew Miss Wood meant it as a kind of compliment to me, but it rankled Fran when the note she received on *her* lesson plans was, "Karen will show you how to write a lesson plan."

Teaching is hard work. You have to be a great actor, motivational speaker, intercessor, interpreter, and referee, who can also name the capitals of all fifty states, unpack the Pythagorean Theorem three ways, and explain why a loving and omnipotent God allows evil to exist.

And all of this happens so publicly. One of the most shockingly brave statements a teacher can utter is "I don't know," and it may be even harder to say to our colleagues than to our students. But in a world where some say human knowledge is doubling every sixteen months, the admission of ignorance has to be one of the most necessary answers in a teacher's arsenal.

Miss Wood thought she was arranging for Fran to learn something from me about writing acceptable lesson plans, but as it turned out what she really did was provide an opportunity for me to learn the real grace of vulnerability that Fran revealed by asking me for help. It is a grace that is always available to teachers but is mostly smothered by the daily business of coping with the buckets of eels that are our students.

In this case, however, Fran's exposing her own ignorance about how to accomplish this particular task allowed ever-present grace to shine through. I use the word "expose" deliberately when describing Fran's brave question, as it illuminates the standard operating procedure of the particular grace she shared.

Like Fran's grace, the *auroras borealis* and *australis*, the great Northern and Southern Lights, are startlingly lovely and always present, yet rarely beheld. The crackling charged solar particles that comprise these Lights swirl constantly all around our atmosphere. The potential is there over the entire planet for the electrons and protons of the solar winds to interact with the Earth's magnetic field and produce the undulating milky greens, mesmerizing violets, and sultry blue waves that the Cree people call the "Dance of the Spirits," but only people in the polar regions of the planet get to behold them. They enjoy this opportunity only because the magnetic shield that protects the Earth is stretched to its thinnest and most penetrable at the poles, allowing the charged solar bits to collide with portions of our upper atmosphere and "excite it," as the physicists say, into the frenzy of light and color that inspires poetry and music in those who behold it and envy in those who can only experience the phenomenon vicariously through photographs and videos. The vulnerability of the Earth's insulating shields makes that astonishing beauty possible.

Fran was oozing with amazing ideas for bringing complex scientific ideas to life for her students. She harnessed their need to move into a brilliant sequence within her "Bug Unit," where they replicated the distinct dances that insects do to notify one another of danger, food, and mating season. Kids linked arms in tight "chromosomal hugs" to drive home the nature of molecular bonding. They created voluptuous abstract watercolor paintings in their study of diffusion across permeable membranes. Fran was a woman brimming with imagination and zest who merely had to learn one new skill in order to be able to package her considerable teaching gifts in a way that made them comprehensible to our principal.

And so she asked me for help in writing an "acceptable" lesson plan. She didn't have to. She knew she was reaching her students. Her actual practice was not going to change, just the way she presented it on paper. It would have been easy for her to ignore Miss Wood's clumsy request and continue to pour her energy into creating rich learning experiences for her students, but instead she humbled herself in order to better serve those students.

Fran chose to say, "I don't know how to do this; would you please help me?" And that voluntary thinning of her protective shield allowed the two of us to enter into a conversation that evolved into a robust, reciprocal relationship. I may never get to see the Northern or Southern Lights in person, but beholding Fran's example of vulnerability invited me to be just as spellbound, dazzled by her grace.

Ninety-Nine Times Out of Ten

Do not fear, for I have redeemed you;
I have called you by name,
you are mine.

ISAIAH 43:1

My husband's mother likes to begin Important Life Lessons with the phrase "ninety-nine times out of ten." One fall evening when I was seasoning our chicken tandoori dinner with a rant about how once again one of the students at school would not bend his actions to my benevolent will and how scurrilously another teacher was treating her teaching partner, my husband Mark reminded me about Jarrod and how, ninety-nine times out of ten, the most wonderful students fall through the cracks, even though we don't want them to.

We had just begun to date, Mark and I. Those heady months coincided with my new job as the religion and math teacher for the middle school grades at a Catholic school. Like substitute teachers, new teachers are often approached as raw meat, and my homeroom class was untiring in its efforts to see if I "meant what I said and said what I meant," as my principal liked to put it during our weekly please-make-it-better sessions. Mark was getting an earful of eighth-grade pranks and could have picked any one of the perps out of a lineup, given my thorough descriptions of them and my litany of their attempts to crack me.

He knew, for instance, that Jesse had used his considerable

computer skills to re-program our classroom printer to substitute "X" everywhere a student had typed "E" on the original document. For a while, he got our default font to be "Zapf Dingbats." Mark could also finger Liam as the most likely planter of at least seven stink bombs that had emptied our wing of the school onto the playground. The Evil Twins, Nick and Joe, had conspired to wad up marshmallows in most of the girls' sports shoes for phys ed in the racks at the back of the room. Trevor had taken to writing with his left (that is, non-dominant) hand, rendering it all illegible.

And it wasn't just the boys with whom he was getting acquainted during my laments. The drama of fourteen-year-old girls was clear to him as well. He could name every member of the Gang of Four, the girls who were the ruling elite in the classroom. They were subtler than the boys, relying mostly on psychological warfare, the kind that left no fingerprints but lots of tears, and Mark knew each of their strategies.

Yes, Mark knew just about all my students by name and offense, because that was the way I usually framed my answers to his kind question, "How was your week?" Occasionally I threw out a few positive bones about this one great kid who often hung around to talk and help me clean up the classroom and loved to read Garrison Keillor and could quote almost all of *Casablanca*. This kid made lists of Latin and Greek root words just for kicks and inserted quirky neologisms he coined from them into his writing. Once I might even have read aloud to Mark a portion of a stellar story problem the boy had written in our algebra class, a problem that was a piece of art, not just a way to set up solving for x.

But I dove right back into relaying the exploits of Jesse, Liam, Trevor, and the Gang of Four after those glossed-over mentionings of one nameless kid's courtliness and intellectual gifts.

My husband comes from a large extended family that held a huge holiday party each winter for over a hundred people. It was a great way to meet his whole family, all at once. We worked the room, and I strove to keep all the names and relationships straight. Then there was a polite tap on my shoulder: "Miz Eifler, what are you doing here?" I turned to find myself face to face with Jarrod, The World's Best Eighth-Grade Boy, who had worked the very un-eighth-grade word "physiognomy" into a sentence just that past week. Mark acted suprised and said, "I didn't know you knew my very cool cousin Jarrod." And how could Mark know I knew Jarrod, since I had never bothered to attach a name to the one student who wasn't giving me professional ulcers?

It's a wearying fact that we teachers over-torment ourselves over a handful of stink-bomb detonators. That is unfortunate. Because in the bigger picture, most of the precious souls who wind up in our classrooms and deserve to have their stories trumpeted are more like Jarrod, ninety-nine times out of ten.

The Rockets' Red Glare

When Jesus saw his mother
and the disciple whom he loved
standing beside her,
he said to his mother,
"Woman, here is your son."
Then he said to the disciple,
"Here is your mother."

JOHN 19:26-27

"You really can't be considered a real teacher until some-one has thrown up in your classroom, and my students hurling half-digested peaches is exactly what happened today." A few heads turned as first-year teacher Tracy made this assertion to me in a crowded craft store line not long ago. Public talk of barfing does tend to capture people's attention. But in the Really Big Picture, Tracy was absolutely right: The teachers students treasure most are those who stood with us in our most frag-ile moments, who helped us clean up the mess in our spirits—as well, perhaps, as the mess on the floor.

Señora McDonald, the ancient Spanish teacher at our Catho-lic elementary school, did just that for Heidi on a day none of us forgot. There was a school-wide spirit assembly, and Heidi had been tapped to sing the national anthem right after the opening prayer. Of course Heidi was chosen; she sang soprano with a se-lective city choral ensemble and we'd all seen her in *Oklahoma!* as

Laurey and in *The Music Man* as Marian the Librarian. The students were their adolescent worst selves as the whole school gathered at a special Friday assembly, with lots of secret rejoicing by both students and faculty for the shortened class periods that would hasten us all into the weekend.

Old bleachers creaked as young bodies still getting used to gangly limbs created a little tremor in their rising to attention, but the mood was generally respectful and nearly everyone remembered to remove their baseball caps. Heidi glided to the microphone stand at the free-throw line of the cafegymatorium. A school piano, slightly on the twangy side, played four measures of the opening to "The Star-Spangled Banner," followed by another four measures, and another, while Heidi took deep breaths and sang...nothing.

The pianist changed keys, but eight more measures of introduction made no difference at all. Standing stock still, Heidi just stared at the entire school body as we all felt a horrible frisson, a shudder of group electricity working its way through the cavernous space.

This awkwardness probably lasted less than a minute, but that is approximately sixteen hours in stage-paralysis time, and as the hushed tension lost its grip, the snickering and whispering took over.

All the teachers and administrators were frozen, all save one. Click, click, click—we heard Señora McDonald's four-inch black patent leather stilettos stride purposefully across the shiny wooden floor. Señora was a *bona fide* school institution who had been teaching Spanish there since the earth was cooling, all 6'4" of her. There had never been a confirmed sighting of her in any natural hair color beyond a flaming auburn beehive, nor was she known to appear in public without a Diet Cola in her hand. She must have had a first name besides Señora, but no one knew what that might be, not even those of us who were her colleagues for years.

We all watched in jaw-dropped awe as her long legs moved her swiftly across the gym floor and next to Heidi. She drew the little girl into a hug against her own pink and purple hound's-tooth check suit, murmured something into her ear, nodded to the pianist, and started singing the national anthem in a quivery soprano that we might have giggled at if we hadn't been stunned at her bravery. Some of the teacher's energy flowed into Heidi, who finally found her own voice somewhere around "the twilight's last gleaming."

When the anthem ended, the two embraced. Every one of us was intimidated by Señora McDonald's simultaneous contact with several hundred pairs of eyes in the room that said, "I absolutely forbid you to make fun of this sweet brave girl when this is over."

And no one did. The assembly's intended content got under-way, happened, was finished, and we all went home for the weekend.

I don't remember a word of what the principal or cheerleaders or student council reps said that day nor—I'm sure—do they. But I can clearly see Heidi, with nearly all her crushed spirit restored, walking over to her seat on the trail blazed for her by those shiny black high heels.

Señora McDonald was a real teacher indeed, just as first-year teacher Tracy had discovered about herself.

Bury as Useful

My brothers and sisters,
whenever you face trials of any kind,
consider it nothing but joy.

JAMES 1:2

My friend Kevin has a great exercise for getting his English students to write more vibrantly. On a Monday in early October, he dons a solemn face and grants the class a moment of silence to mourn the death of the words "good," "bad," and "boring." Kevin announces that these three words—having died—are no longer available for use in student prose or class discussions. Kevin then employs his flair for the dramatic as he affixes to the front wall three Styrofoam tombstones (acquired for a dollar after the Halloween season was over one year) with the "dead" words engraved under an enormous RIP at the top of each.

But since it is obvious that the concepts "good," "bad," and "boring" still need to be expressed, his classes next spend time combing thesauruses for synonyms for each word and analyzing how professional critics communicate the three concepts. In the process, his students learn enduring lessons about connotation and denotation.

Subsequent months see Kevin's students infusing the fruits of all that labor into reinvigorated book reports and essays. Their favorite fiction is no longer "good," but "delectable," and "bad" love poems are now deemed "lugubrious" by formerly reluctant and insecure writers.

It occurred to the entire faculty when Kevin was describing this simple teaching tip at an afternoon "best shot seminar" over tar-like coffee in our "lounge" that some other words really do need to be buried. Not because of their blandness, which was Kevin's inspiration, but because Elie Wiesel was absolutely right when he said, "We become our words." So each of us agreed to bid farewell to a word or phrase of our own that kept us from doing our best teaching.

Fear was Lucy's candidate for burial. She quoted poet Mary Anne Radmacher that courage doesn't always roar. Sometimes courage is the small voice inside that says, "I will try again tomorrow." We all 'fessed up that one of the things we most feared was facing our students and peers after a "bad" (or should I say, "lugubrious") day. We recalled that "Do not be afraid" was one of Jesus' favorite greetings to his disciples, especially to those cowering behind locked doors, unwilling to risk human contact. Once the fear was gone, their only limits were "the ends of the earth." Now *that* is a way for teachers to confront a month of Mondays!

Finished was Sister Marge's word that needed burying. "We never are finished," she said, "even after our most stellar lessons. What's more, we're not finished after our most scandalously awful lessons either, even though we tend to put our failures on infinite replay while forgetting our successes with students as easily as we forget the score of last night's Laker game."

The day's last gravestone was reserved for the phrase *just a teacher*, as in "I'm just a teacher." This was Marilyn's contribution. "In any given week," she said, "every teacher here serves as a theologian, orator, arbitrator, confidante, coach, counselor, medic, traffic cop, pharmacist, referee, social worker, comedian, legislator, executive, judge, editor, healer of broken hearts, critic, and motivational speaker, regardless of the content area you teach." She reminded us that when a neurosurgeon gets the sniffles, his or her surgeries for the day are cancelled, and the same goes for astronauts and plenty of other occupations. But what we teachers do is so vital that when one of us can't be in school, a "substitute" must be hired immediately to keep the learning and the caring and the healing moving forward.

"To teachers!" We all hoisted our Styrofoam cups.
It was my favorite funeral ever.

Falling in Love Again

*Listen, I will tell
you a mystery!
We will not all die,
but we will all be changed,
in a moment,
in the twinkling of an eye,
at the last trumpet.*

1 CORINTHIANS 15:51-52

Thirteen-year-old girls swampled in graduation gowns and teetering on their first high heels down the aisle of a cafe-gymatorium are so beautiful. So are their male classmates, flaunting their gaudy first ties and nursing blisters in dress shoes encasing feet that have mostly only known sneakers.

What makes our students especially lovely is the look on each face as they search the audience for the dearest faces in their worlds—those of their parents, grandparents, and siblings—faces that, for the moment and for the same reason, are just as beautiful as theirs. If someone could bottle pure in-spite-of-everything-familial-love, they would have the best cosmetic ever invented.

It's no wonder, then, that "Pomp and Circumstance" is the soundtrack for so many commercials aimed right at our hearts. There is something about graduation ceremonies, even in eighth grade, that can crack open the stoniest teacher heart and keep an exhausted teacher signing on for another year. Here is why I think we all go through so many tissues each June.

Every parent falls in love with an infant and then has to say goodbye to that infant in order to fall in love with a one-year-old, only to have that baby turn into a two-year-old, who gives way to a three-year-old, and so on and so forth. The same thing happens with teachers.

At the end of every school year, and especially at the end of the "big" years, like the first and third and fifth and eighth and twelfth and sixteenth—every teacher dies a little. We have to "let the dead bury the dead" and fall in love again with a whole new group of children. Luckily, we are able to do so, but there are an awful lot of goodbyes that have to take place first.

Whether we teach elementary school or middle school or high school or college, it doesn't really matter—we have to say goodbye to that chubby little guy we grew to love or that awkward, dreamy little girl who always made us smile or the gangly kid who just barely passed our class.

All of these students leave, although if we are lucky we will catch glimpses of them throughout their lives. But their exasperating, captivating, hilarious, fragile, resilient thirteen-year-old selves are gone forever. So when they leave us, although we know we will fall in love with the next group, first we must brace for the sorrow of another necessary goodbye to those precious persons we had only recently (and in some cases only finally) begun figuring out.

That might explain the many lumps surprising our collective throats and the slight tingling on the corners of so many of our eyes at the end of each school year, which we never would have expected because we have been waiting for months for this particular class to graduate so we can shake their dust from our sandals.

It's not hard to understand why many female veterans of annual graduations know not to wear mascara (it will run) and remember to stock up on Kleenex before the procession begins. Graduation ceremonies afford us all a chance to stop what we are doing, treasure precious memories, mourn a real loss, and prepare to fall in love with a brand new group of young people we didn't think we had room for in our hearts.

But we can, and we do, and we will.

ACKNOWLEDGMENTS

I have been crazy blessed to learn from the most gifted teachers on the planet, starting with my parents, Clyde and Marilyn, and continuing on through Sister Florette Marie, Joan, Pierre, Mary Jo, Bruce, Jim, Dennis, Tom, Charlie, Virginia, and my wondrous son, Conor. Thanks to Pat and Brian for triple-dog-daring me and to Greg, first for the idea of making this book a month of Mondays and second for making it elegant. I also appreciate the creative artistry of Patricia and Tom on the design and production.

I remember auditing a graduate course taught by a man who made the hours fly by through his animation, command of an astonishing number of ideas, and palpable kindness. As I was taking notes, I found myself wishing I could get to know him better, and then I had to laugh: I was married to him! But he is such a gifted teacher that I actually forgot we were married, so far into the stories of the Great Plains Native Americans had he transported all of us in that room. How could this book not be for Mark?

PS 46